STUMPWORK EMBROIDERY & THREAD PAINTING

Stitch 3-D Nature Motifs

MEGAN ZANIEWSKI

stashBOOKS.
an imprint of C&T Publishing

PUBLISHER | Amy Barrett-Daffin

CREATIVE DIRECTOR | Gailen Runge

SENIOR EDITOR | Roxane Cerda

EDITOR | Madison Moore

TECHNICAL EDITOR | Kathryn Patterson

COVER/BOOK DESIGNER | April Mostek

PRODUCTION COORDINATOR | Zinnia Heinzmann

ILLUSTRATOR | Aliza Shalit

PHOTOGRAPHY COORDINATOR | Rachel Ackley

FRONT COVER PHOTOGRAPHY by Elizabeth James

INSTRUCTIONAL AND SUBJECT PHOTOGRAPHY by Megan Zaniewski

LIFESTYLE PHOTOGRAPHY by Elizabeth James, unless otherwise noted

Published by Stash Books, an imprint of C&T Publishing, Inc., P.O. Box 1456, Lafayette, CA 94549

Library of Congress Cataloging-in-Publication Data

Names: Zaniewski, Megan, 1987- author.

Title: Stumpwork embroidery & thread painting : stitch 3-D nature motifs / Megan Zaniewski.

Description: Lafayette : Stash Books, an imprint of C&T Publishing, [2024] | Summary: "Embroidery reaches a new level of excitement with Megan Zaniewski's stumpwork embroidery techniques. In this book of nature-inspired pieces and projects, with step-by-step instructions, stitchers will learn to use thread painting, stunning finishing techniques, and 3-D elements to make their embroidery leap off the fabric"-- Provided by publisher.

Identifiers: LCCN 2023030674 | ISBN 9781644034149 (trade paperback) | ISBN 9781644034156 (ebook)

Subjects: LCSH: Embroidery--Patterns. | Textile painting. | Nature in art.

Classification: LCC TT771 .Z36 2024 | DDC 746.44/041--dc23/eng/20230724

LC record available at https://lccn.loc.gov/2023030674

Printed in the USA

10 9 8 7 6 5 4 3 2

Dedication

For Maya, Claire, and Ian, whose limitless imaginations and curiosity inspire me to look in wonder at the world every day; and for Lee, whose love and support made this dream possible.

Acknowledgments

The challenges of writing a book were eased by the unwavering support of so many people, for which I am forever grateful.

Thank you to my parents whose love and encouragement gave me the foundation and confidence needed to reach for my goals. JP, thank you for sharing your reverence for nature with me and teaching me the joy of creating. Mom, thank you for encouraging me to pick up a needle and thread in the first place and to pursue art seriously. (I also appreciate you sharing your extensive fabric and thread collection with me).

Cal, thank you for making me laugh through it all and for being there always, even from 1500 miles away.

Thank you to my editor, Madison, and the amazing team at C&T Publishing for seeing potential in me and bringing this book to life. Your contagious enthusiasm and patient hand-holding made the entire process truly enjoyable.

Thank you to Karen, Cass, Lyndsi, Sarah V., Jen, Jessica, Varsha, Jennifer, Ruthie, Katie, Hope, Kayla, Emily, Laura, Carrie, Christa, Alana, Laney, Melina, Meg, Erin, Susanna, Sarah L., Ed, and so many others in the fiber arts community on Instagram. Your kind support bolstered me through the vulnerable and self-doubting moments of creating and writing for an audience.

Thank you to the Audubon Center in Moss Point for allowing me to access and photograph their nest specimens for inspiration for the Robin's Nest pattern.

Special thanks to Marco and Betty at ArtBase, Renae and the Benzie Design team, Colonial Needle Company, and Nurge for generously supplying the materials I needed to embroider the projects in this book.

Contents

Introduction

I am so glad you've picked up this book. I've written it for kindred spirits: those who marvel at the beauty of nature, appreciate the feel of a needle and thread between their fingers, and seek the fulfillment that comes with creating something magical with their own hands.

The projects in this book introduce you to thread painting and stumpwork embroidery techniques. You'll learn how to embroider realistic plants and animals by blending thread colors as a painter blends paint, create depth with padded foundations, add texture with different fibers, and create height with wire slips. The animals and plants you embroider with these step-by-step patterns will truly seem to come to life, stitch by stitch.

It is my hope that these techniques open up a world of creative possibilities for you. By completing the patterns in this book, you will gain the skills and confidence needed to embroider your own original designs. There is no shortage of inspiration to be found in the natural world, and there is no limit to your imagination. So, this book is your invitation to explore new techniques, have fun, and think outside the hoop. I hope you enjoy using this book as much as I have enjoyed writing it for you. Happy stitching!

Finding Inspiration in Nature

Nature is everywhere. Even when we are immersed in our daily life and feel far removed from nature, it appears in simple and often unremarkable ways—a ladybug wanders into your home, a leaf sticks to your shoe, birdsong outside the window fills the morning. Look and listen. Finding inspiration in nature requires only a quiet pause to observe your surroundings.

My embroideries are largely inspired by these daily observations of nature and the questions that arise from them. What do you wonder about the animals or plants you observe? If you've held a buttercup, have you ever questioned why the petals appear to shimmer and glow in the sunshine? Have you wondered what materials the robin uses to make its nest? Asking questions about the animals and plants you observe draws you closer to them as subjects, and as you learn more, you can explore ways to convey that understanding in your art, through various combinations of texture and technique.

In this book, I guide you step by step through fifteen embroidery projects with three-dimensional elements and share insights on how to develop your own nature-inspired motifs.

Stumpwork Embroidery

The term *stumpwork* refers broadly to a wide variety of three-dimensional embroidery techniques. This book covers a few of them and demonstrates how to apply them to embroider realistic animal and botanical portraits that dramatically emerge from their frames.

Embroidery with a wire slip is featured heavily in this book's projects. Wire slips can take any shape and are great for making wings and flower petals. After they are embroidered, the embellished wire slips are attached to an embroidered base. These striking 3-D elements help bring realistic embroideries to life. Butterflies appear ready to fly off the fabric, and flowers seem to bloom out of their frames.

Padded stumpwork is another of the varieties we'll cover. It's the process of layering felt pieces onto a fabric base to form a raised shape to embroider on. This technique adds depth and dimension to an embroidered subject.

| *The Hummingbird (page 116) flies out of the frame with a wire slip wing.*

The Mallard Duckling (page 37) uses embroidery on padded felt layers to shape the body and achieve subtle depth.

Thread Painting

The term *thread painting* refers to an embroidery technique that blends different colors of thread in a mix of long and short stitches, similar to blending paint with brushstrokes. This technique allows the artist to create shadows and depth to embroider realistic portraits. This book shows how thread painting can be used to create highly detailed embroideries of animal and botanical subjects.

The Monarch Butterfly (page 47) combines thread painting with wire slip wings.

Tools and Materials

General Embroidery Materials

Fabric

In general, look for fabric that has a tight, even weave whenever you're making a project with thread painting. Fabrics with too much stretch or large, uneven weaves may distort when put in an embroidery hoop, resulting in a finished embroidery that is wrinkled or messy looking.

COTTON

My preferred fabric for embroidery is 100% cotton. I look for a high thread count, usually 60 × 60 or 60 × 75 threads per inch. Higher thread counts enable you to achieve greater detail in thread painting. I recommend Robert Kaufman's Kona Cotton Solids line. It is widely available in most fabric stores and online, and it comes in 365 colors, so it is easy to find the perfect shade to complement your subject.

FELT

High-quality wool felt is important for padded stumpwork. Lower-quality acrylic blend felt tears and stretches too easily, and the rough texture can wear down more delicate threads. I recommend Benzie's wool blend felt and 100% merino wool felt for padded stumpwork projects. These felts hold their shape and come in precut sheets in a wide range of colors that can easily be matched to your subject.

Embroidery Hoops

I recommend beechwood embroidery hoops for your projects. Nurge makes high-quality beechwood hoops in many sizes. They hold the fabric drum tight and do not lose tension as you stitch. The smooth edges are also gentle on your hands.

Nurge also makes plastic hoops for displaying finished embroideries. Their faux-wood flexi hoops are an easy solution for giving your embroidery a beautiful framed look without the extra steps of framing.

Needles

EMBROIDERY

Embroidery needles are best used with cotton embroidery floss and some specialty threads, such as fine metallic braid. Needles in sizes 9 and 10 are used most commonly for the projects in this book. I recommend the Sharps line of embroidery needles by John James.

TAPESTRY AND CHENILLE

I use tapestry and chenille needles for embroidering with wider fibers, such as silk ribbons and tapestry wool. I also use them for attaching wire slips to base fabric. I recommend the Tapestry and Chenille line of embroidery needles by John James.

Scissors

You need two types of scissors for embroidery: fabric scissors and thread scissors. Fabric scissors, sometimes called dressmaker scissors, are designed for cutting fabric. They are 7˝–10˝ (17.8–25.4cm) long, with a flat lower blade that glides easily along the cutting surface and leaves the cut fabric with clean edges. Thread scissors are about 3˝–4˝ (7.6–10.2cm) long, with short blades that are angled to a sharp point. They are best suited for small, precise snipping.

Materials for Transferring Patterns

GRAPHITE TRANSFER PAPER

Graphite transfer paper is easy to use and accurately transfers highly detailed designs to light and dark fabrics. Use white graphite paper for dark fabrics and black graphite paper for light fabrics. Once transferred, the design is permanent, so trace with care. See Transferring Patterns (page 27) for more on how to use graphite transfer paper.

FABRIC PENS AND PENCILS

Water- and air-soluble pens are a nonpermanent option for transferring designs onto light-colored fabrics. They are quick and easy to use, but the blunt tip on most pens is not ideal for transferring highly detailed or miniature designs.

Mechanical chalk pencils, such as Bohin's mechanical chalk pencil, can nicely transfer designs to darker fabrics. The finer tip also allows you to draw in greater detail. Chalk can sometimes rub away before you want it to, so you may need to touch up the design throughout the embroidery process.

PRINT AND STICK PAPER

Sulky Stick 'n Stitch paper and C&T Publishing's Wash-Away Stitch Stabilizer offer an effortless way to transfer designs. Simply print the design onto the water-soluble sticker paper from your home printer, peel away the sticker back, and adhere the sticker to the fabric. After you embroider the design, wash the paper away. Be sure to carefully read the paper instructions for your specific printer to ensure that the ink will not run and stain the fabric. And always check that your threads are colorfast if you plan to use this method. See Transferring Patterns (page 27) for more on how to use this paper.

Thread

SIX-STRANDED COTTON

Six-stranded cotton embroidery floss is the most popular and accessible thread for embroidery. It comes in thousands of colors, solid and variegated. It is made of six strands of thread that can be separated. You can stitch with all six strands for a very textured look, or you can split the thread and use fewer strands for smoother, detailed work. Most of the projects in this book require you to split the thread to just one or two strands to capture high levels of detail. When selecting cotton embroidery floss, look for high-quality, colorfast threads, such as those from DMC and Anchor.

SEWING

Cotton sewing thread is finer than even one strand of cotton embroidery floss, which makes it great for adding very small details, especially in miniature designs. Gütermann all-purpose cotton sewing thread is a high-quality colorfast thread that blends well with regular cotton embroidery floss.

SPECIALTY

I use the term *specialty thread* to refer to any threads that are not standard cotton, including metallic or iridescent threads, silk, and wool blends. These threads are often delicate and require a little more care when used in embroidery, but they can add dramatic texture and visual interest to a piece.

TAPESTRY YARN

Tapestry yarn is a thick, single-ply wool yarn that is traditionally embroidered onto canvas, but it can also be used on tighter-weave fabrics, such as cotton and linen. It adds a lot of texture and character to an embroidery project, so it is great for whimsical designs. It is soft enough to embroider onto clothing and looks great on accessories, including tote bags, hats, and aprons.

Jewelry Bezels and Frames

Picking a setting for your embroidery is an important part of the design process. A frame should complement your design without overwhelming it.

JEWELRY SETTINGS

Jewelry settings allow you to turn your embroideries into accessories. They come in a wide variety of sizes, shapes, and materials, so it is easy to find one that fits your subject and style. Some settings come with a *bezel*, a fitted insert to help secure the embroidery to the setting. If it does not, you can make one yourself from a piece of mat board or cardboard. Trace the inside diameter of the setting on a thin piece of parchment or tracing paper, cut out the traced shape, and then use it as a template to trace and cut a matching piece of mat board to fit inside the setting.

FRAMES

Frames can be either bought new or thrifted. Vintage frames often have unique characteristics that can add visual interest to a finished embroidery, and thrifted frames usually come at a lower price point. Standard store-bought frames are more widely available.

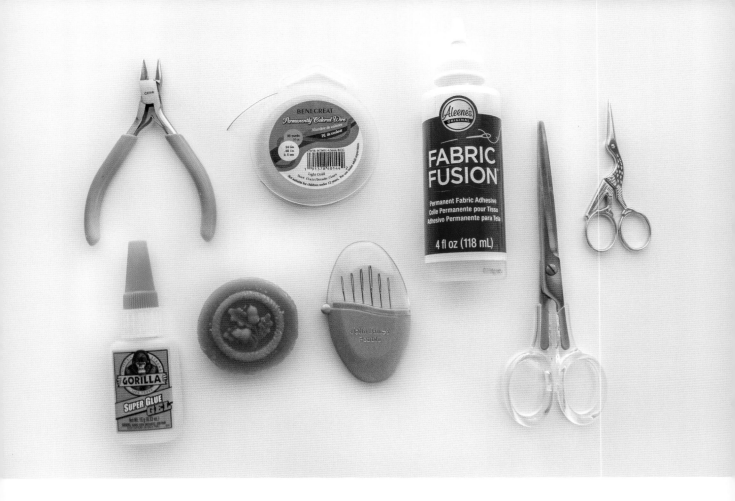

Stumpwork Materials

Wire and Cutters

Jewelry wire is used to create wire-slip elements that pop out from the embroidered base. A thin wire, such as 24 gauge, is easily manipulated and best used for crafting into very detailed shapes. Look for coated or rust-resistant wire that will not corrode over time. You will also need wire cutters to trim it.

Glue

Secure the edges and backside of a wire-slip embroidery with fabric glue, such as Aleene's Fabric Fusion. Secure embroideries in jewelry settings with superglue. Any brand of superglue should be suitable for metal and wood settings, but I prefer to use Loctite Super Glue Ultra Liquid Control because it allows you to precisely control the amount of glue that comes out. This quality is beneficial when working with small settings.

Thread Conditioner

Strengthen and smooth embroidery floss that is wrapped around wire slips with a beeswax thread conditioner. The conditioner prevents tangling and fraying.

Color and Design

From inspiration to final framing, the process of creating a finished piece incorporates many color and design choices. In this chapter, I walk you through the steps I take to design a piece so you can create a one-of-a-kind piece of your own.

Subjects and References

Begin with a model, live sketch, or photograph of your subject. Multiple references allow you to better understand your subject and its unique characteristics.

Models of a subject can vary widely: a toy figurine of an animal, a preserved animal in a natural science museum, and a specimen collected outdoors (nests, shells, flowers, and so forth) are just a few examples. Models can help you understand where to add volume with padded stumpwork, 3-D elements with wire slips, and shadows with thread painting to make your embroidery appear true to life.

A real nest abandoned in a nesting box at a local bird center serves as inspiration and a model for drafting a miniature embroidery design.

Keeping a small notebook at hand while outdoors can be a great tool for designing your own nature motifs, even if drawing is not your strength. Sketches based on observations from life can be quick and messy. Drawing the subject perfectly is unimportant. The idea is simply to capture inspiration when it strikes! A doodle with a few words about texture or light can help jog your memory later when you begin planning an embroidery.

You can also take photos or browse royalty-free photography websites for images of a desired subject. Photos are very helpful for matching thread colors to your subject and drafting an outline for the embroidery pattern. They're also great for studying subjects that are not native to your area. Choose photos with natural, even lighting to avoid mismatching thread colors.

Creating a Pattern

Once you've chosen a subject and gathered some inspiration or reference, draw a freehand outline of the subject or trace a reference photograph. Identify the features that make the subject recognizable and focus on adding detail in those areas. Which features come to mind when you recall that animal? It may be the furry stripes of a bee, the wing pattern of a butterfly, the puffed cheeks and striped tail of a chipmunk, or the wispy feathers of a duckling. Emphasize the details of these areas in your design, and the final embroidery will be more lifelike. Draw your sketches digitally or on paper.

Triangular Composition

Consider the overall composition of your pattern. Creating a triangular composition is a fail-proof way to ensure that your design is balanced and visually appealing. For example, consider the Broad-Billed Hummingbird Pattern below. The beak of the hummingbird juts out in front, but it is balanced by the extended tail feathers on the opposite side. Likewise, the wing bisects the negative space around the hummingbird and completes a triangular composition. Alone, these features might disrupt the negative space. But viewed together, they create harmony and balance.

In this digital sketch of a duckling, the main features are outlined with simple, bold lines. The fluffy feathers are the most detailed part of the pattern because they are the duckling's most identifiable feature.

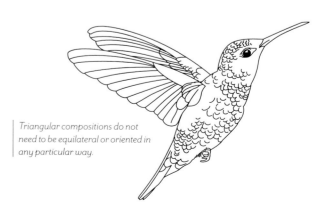

Triangular compositions do not need to be equilateral or oriented in any particular way.

Framing

Before you start embroidering, also consider how the composition of the design will look in its final frame. A design should be centered in its frame, with enough negative space around the embroidery to ensure that the piece doesn't look crowded. Wire-slip elements, such as wings and petals, should overextend the frame by about 1″ (2.5cm) or less for the most balanced look.

Designing Stumpwork Elements

When designing a three-dimensional embroidery element, consider the subject's anatomy. For example, if you are embroidering an animal subject, consider which of the animal's body parts would look most striking in 3-D. For many animals, such as insects and birds, embroidered wings provide that "wow" factor. If you are embroidering flowers, petals are often the part that stands out the most.

Combine traditional embroidery with multiple stumpwork techniques to create a range of depth. For example, the antennae of the Rosy Maple Moth are embroidered flat against the base fabric. The body is elevated above the antennae with padding and turkey stitches, and the wings rise even higher above the body with wire slips. Include two or more levels of depth in a design to create a more striking three-dimensional effect.

Selecting Materials

Let the subject inform your materials. Embroidering a bird's nest? Work with natural fibers and a mixture of rough and soft textures. Embroidering flowers? Consider delicate silk ribbons. You can explore a wide variety of specialty fibers to help draw attention to the unique characteristics of your subject. Do not let unfamiliarity with a certain fiber deter you from trying something new. Experimenting with new textures can be a fun next step in your embroidery journey.

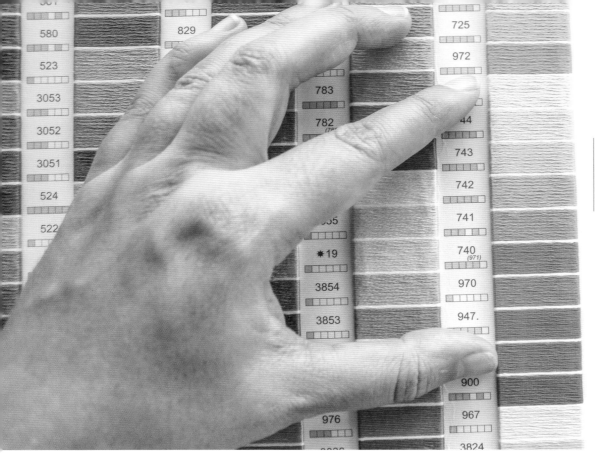

The DMC Threaded Color Card displays colors in a clear gradient, beginning with the lightest tint and ending with the darkest shade.

Selecting Thread Colors

The DMC Threaded Color Card is a useful tool for picking harmonious thread colors and matching them to a reference photograph. Threads are organized in rows of color families on the card. Each row is further divided into gradients of four to ten colors. This organized system takes the guesswork out of picking thread colors that blend seamlessly together with long and short stitches. Simply select thread colors from the same gradient group or row for a harmonious palette.

If you do not have a DMC Threaded Color Card, you can also look at thread numbers to easily identify gradients. The thread numbers within a gradient run in numerical order. With DMC thread, the smallest number correlates to the darkest shade in the gradient, and the largest number correlates to the lightest shade. Anchor threads are ordered the opposite way, with the lightest tint as the smallest number.

Selecting Fabric Color

Picking a base fabric color that complements your thread color palette will help your embroidery stand out. Guide your choice with a color wheel; I like using the Essential Color Wheel Companion by Joen Wolfrom. First, identify the dominant thread colors in your pattern on the color wheel. Then, follow one of the suggested color scheme options for selecting the fabric color.

For more fail-proof color selections, I also like to refer to the Ultimate 3-in-1 Color Tool by Joen Wolfrom. Its preset color schemes and recommendations for color groupings can help you pick the best fabric color for your project.

COMPLEMENTARY COLORS

Complementary colors lie opposite each other on the color wheel. Luna Moth's dominant colors fall in the spring-green family. Fuchsia is opposite spring green on the color wheel, so I selected a fuchsia base fabric for a beautiful color pairing that helps the moth stand out.

SPLIT-COMPLEMENTARY COLORS

To create a split-complementary color scheme, you must first identify an analogous color scheme within the pattern. *Analogous colors* are colors that are next to each other on the color wheel. Then, pair these colors with a complementary color. For example, the analogous colors that are used in Monarch Butterfly are orange-red, orange, yellow-orange, orange-yellow, and golden yellow. Cerulean blue is the complementary color opposite this color scheme on the color wheel. So, I paired the monarch with a light-tinted hue of cerulean blue.

TRIADIC COLORS

To create a triadic scheme, begin by identifying the dominant thread color. Its triadic partners fall an equal distance from it on the color wheel. For example, the dominant color in Rosy Maple Moth is magenta. Yellow and cyan are its triadic partners, each equidistant from it on the color wheel. These colors are reflected in the secondary thread colors and the fabric color choice.

Displaying Embroidery

Displaying in a Hoop

A hoop is the simplest way to display a finished embroidery. You may need to use
a different size hoop than the one you used while embroidering.

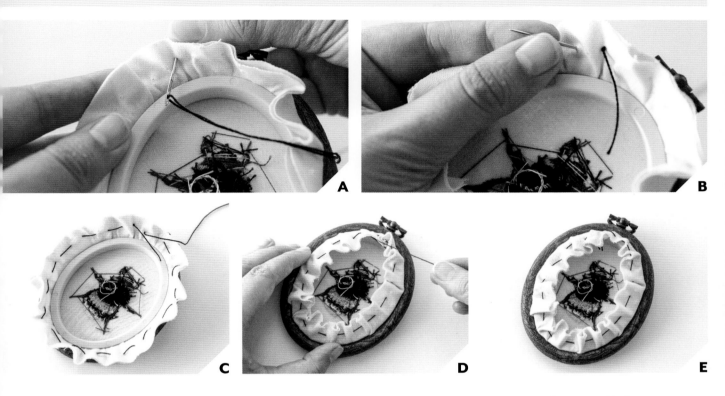

1. Center and secure the embroidery in the hoop. Gently pull the fabric drum tight so the embroidery is wrinkle-free.
Trim away the excess fabric so only a 1¼˝ (3.2cm) border remains.

2. Measure and cut a piece of pearl cotton embroidery thread
(any color) about 3˝ (7.6cm) longer than the length of the hoop's
perimeter. Thread a chenille needle with it.

3. On the backside of the hoop, bring the needle through the
middle of the excess fabric. **A**

4. Make a ⅜˝ (1cm) straight stitch through the excess fabric. **B**

5. Continue to make evenly spaced ⅜˝ (1cm) stitches along the
perimeter of the hoop until reaching the starting stitch. This is
called a running stitch. **C**

6. Gently pull the excess thread to gather the fabric. **D**

7. Knot and trim the excess thread. **E**

Displaying in a Frame

Make sure you have an appropriately sized frame selected before you begin preparing your embroidery. You'll also need an acid-free archival mat board.

A

B

C

D

E

F

G

1. Cut a piece of acid-free archival mat board to fit inside the frame. Center the mat board on the back of the embroidery and outline the shape of the board on the fabric with an air-soluble pen. **A**

2. Measure and cut a piece of pearl cotton embroidery thread (any color) twice the length of the perimeter of the mat board. Thread a chenille needle with it. Stitch a ⅜" (1cm) running stitch (see Steps 3–5 in Displaying in a Hoop, page 23) around the embroidery, about ⅝" (1.6cm) from the edge. Leave the excess thread attached to the needle and fabric. Press the mat board onto the back of the embroidery. **B**

3. Hold the mat board in place. Gently pull the excess thread to gather the fabric around it. **C**

4. Push the needle between the fabric and mat board at any point along the perimeter. **D**

5. Bring the thread across the back of the board to the opposite side and pull the needle through. Repeat until the backside is crisscrossed with thread. Gently pull the

fabric taut with each pass of the needle. This should help flatten the back of the fabric. Tie off the end of the thread. **E**

6. Place the embroidery into the frame and ensure that the design is centered and wrinkle-free. **F**

7. Attach the backing board of the frame. **G**

Displaying in a Jewelry Setting

Make sure that you choose a jewelry setting well suited to the size of the embroidery.

1. Pendant settings often come with a fitted insert, or bezel. If your setting does not come with a bezel, cut a piece of cardboard to fit snugly inside the setting. See Jewelry Settings (page 14). **A**

2. Thread a size 10 needle with one strand of cotton embroidery floss in any color. Follow Steps 1–6 in Displaying in a Frame (page 24). **B**

3. Place the embroidery into the setting. Make sure that it is centered and wrinkle-free. Tighten the setting. **C**

4. Glue the back of the setting to the frame with superglue. **D**

5. Hold for five seconds, or until the glue sets. **E**

Stitches and Techniques

Transferring Patterns

Graphite Transfer Paper

Graphite transfer paper is my preferred method for transferring designs. Black graphite paper is suitable for lighter fabrics, and white graphite paper is suitable for darker fabrics. One sheet of graphite paper can be used multiple times before losing its effectiveness. The downside to this method is that the pattern lines cannot be removed from the fabric.

1. Tape the fabric right side up on a flat surface. Tape a piece of graphite paper over the fabric, with the graphite side facing down. **A**

2. Place the pattern over the graphite paper. Slowly trace each line in the pattern with a fine- or sharp-tipped pen. Use enough pressure to transfer the design clearly, but don't rip the paper. **B**

3. Remove the tape and graphite paper. Check for any mistakes. The pattern is ready to be embroidered! **C**

> **· CORRECTING TRANSFER MISTAKES ·**
>
> *It is important to transfer your pattern carefully because graphite transfer paper is fairly permanent. However, mistakes happen! If you make a mistake when transferring the design, Amodex Ink and Stain Remover can often remove the graphite lines from most fabrics.*

A

B

C

Printable Stick 'n Stitch Paper

Sulky Stick 'n Stitch paper provides a quick and easy way to transfer designs. Keep in mind that this transfer method works only with colorfast threads, such as DMC and Anchor, that do not run when washed.

1. Follow the package instructions to print the design onto the sticker paper with your home printer. Cut around the design, leaving a ½″–1″ (1.2–2.5cm) margin. **D**

2. Peel away the back of the sticker and adhere it to the fabric. Secure the fabric in the hoop and tighten the hoop's hardware until the fabric is drum-tight. **E**

3. Embroider the pattern. After the project is complete, hand wash the paper away in warm, soapy water. Rinse well and air-dry.

D

E

Splitting Six-Stranded Cotton Thread

Cotton embroidery thread is stranded, which means that it is made up of individual threads wound together. Most patterns in this book require you to split the stranded thread down to one or two strands.

To split, gently hold all the threads between two fingers. With your other hand, isolate a single thread and slowly pull upward. The thread should slide free of the other strands without tangling. **A**

A

Threading Silk Ribbon

Silk ribbon is threaded on a needle in a specific way to reduce wear and tear on the delicate ribbon.

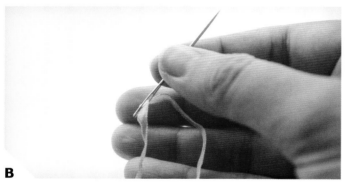

B

C

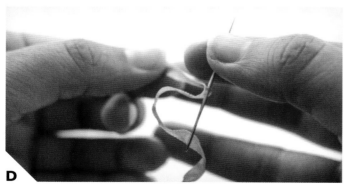

D

E

1. Pull the end of the silk ribbon through the chenille needle. Leave a short tail, about 1˝–1½˝ (2.5–3.8cm) long. **B**

2. Pierce the middle of the ribbon with the needle. **C**

3. Gently pull on the short end of the pierced ribbon, pulling it down the needle. **D**

4. A knot will form at the end of the needle's eye. Tie an additional knot at the long end of the ribbon. **E**

Stitching

The stitches in this section are used in the projects throughout the book. Refer to this section as needed.

Straight Stitch

Keep straight stitches short, no longer than ⅜" (1cm). Multiple straight stitches are called running stitches.

1. Bring the needle up at the starting point of the stitch. **A**

2. Bring the needle back down through the fabric to create the stitch. **B**

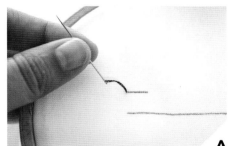

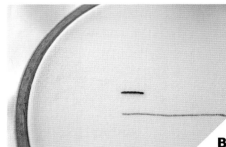

Seed Stitch

Seed stitches are embroidered the same way as straight stitches. The difference between the two stitches is the length. Seed stitches are much smaller, usually only a couple of millimeters long.

1. Follow the instructions for Straight Stitch (above), but make the stitch smaller. **C**

A cluster of seed stitches at various angles

Backstitch

The backstitch is embroidered with a series of equal-length, connected straight stitches.

1. Make a straight stitch. **D**

2. Bring the needle back up through the fabric a stitch-length away from the end of the first stitch. **E**

3. Bring the needle down through the same hole where the first stitch ends. **F**

4. Repeat Steps 2 and 3 until you have completed the line of stitches. **G**

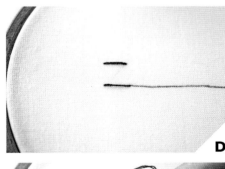

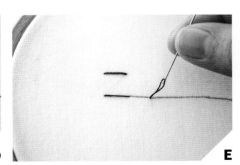

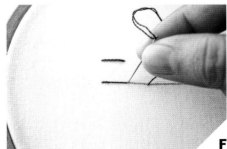

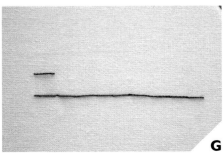

French Knot

The trick to embroidering French knots with ease is maintaining tension on the thread. One hand holds the needle, while the other hand gently grips the working thread to create even tension.

1. Bring the needle up through the fabric at the point where you want the finished knot to be. Drape the thread over the needle. **A**

2. Wrap the thread around the needle once for a small knot. For larger knots, wrap the thread around the needle multiple times. **B**

3. Keep tension on the working thread. Bring the needle down all the way through the fabric, next to the starting point. **C**

4. Pull the thread through to form the knot. **D**

> **· HOOP STAND ·**
>
> *A hoop stand is not a required tool for embroidery, but it can help make two-handed stitches, such as French knots, easier to manage. It can also help alleviate hand strain and keep your hoop from losing fabric tension while you embroider.*

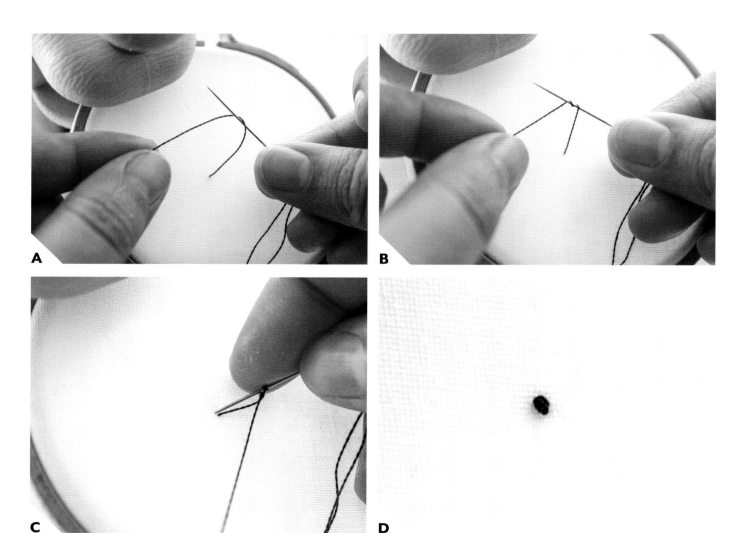

A

B

C

D

Peking Knot

A Peking knot is a loop of thread anchored in one spot by a knot. The loop lays flat against the fabric.

1. Bring the needle up through the fabric at the point where you want the top of the loop to go. This point is where the anchoring knot is made. Shape a loop with the thread close to the starting point. **A**

2. Bring the needle through the loop of thread and all the way down through the fabric, next to the starting point. **B**

3. Gently pull the thread to finish the anchoring stitch at the top of the loop. Do not pull too hard, or the loop of thread will be pulled through the fabric as well. **C**

The size of the thread loop in Step 1 determines the final size of the stitched loop. Make smaller or larger loops by adjusting the size of the loop in Step 1.

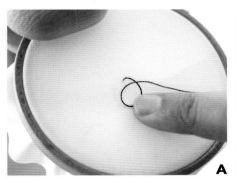

A

B

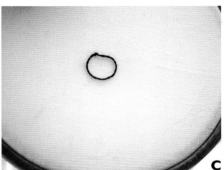

C

Satin Stitch

Satin stitches fill an entire area with thread.

1. Bring the needle up at the top right edge of the area to be filled. **D**

2. Bring the needle down through the fabric directly across from the starting point, creating a straight stitch. **E**

3. Repeat Steps 1 and 2 until the shape is filled. Keep the stitches close together so there are no gaps between them. Always bring the needle up on the same side and back down on the same side so the straight stitches lay flat against the fabric. Change the length of the stitch as needed to fit the shape. **F**

D

E

F

Turkey Stitch

The turkey stitch, or Ghiordes knot, is a three-dimensional stitch that creates a fluffy texture. When embroidering this stitch, I often thread my needle with two shades from the same color family to create extra depth. **A**

1. Bring the needle up at the top edge of the area to be filled. **B**

2. Bring the needle down directly next to the starting point. Do not pull the thread all the way through. Leave a loop of thread about ⅝˝–⅞˝ (1.6–2.2cm) tall on the front side of the work. **C**

3. Bring the needle up between the two points of the loop. **D**

4. Bring the needle down to the right side of the loop. **E**

5. Pull the thread all the way through to create an anchor stitch at the right base of the loop. **F**

6. Repeat Steps 1–5 directly next to the first loop. **G**

7. Continue to fill the shape with anchored loops of thread stitched in rows. **H**

8. Cut through the loops at the top. **I**

9. Trim the threads to the desired height and shape for the project. Gently rub the threads with your finger or a dry, clean toothbrush to fluff and loosen them. **J**

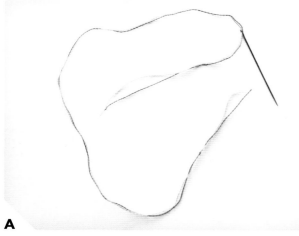

A

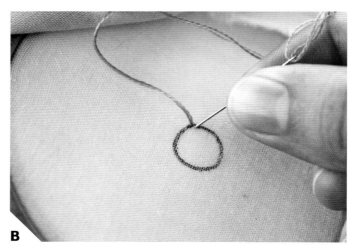

B

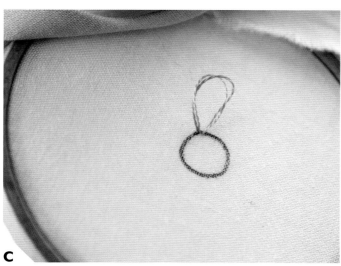

C

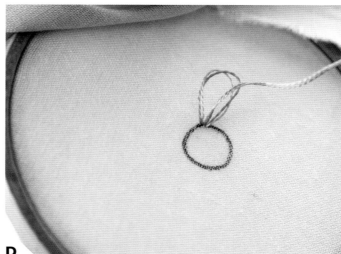

D

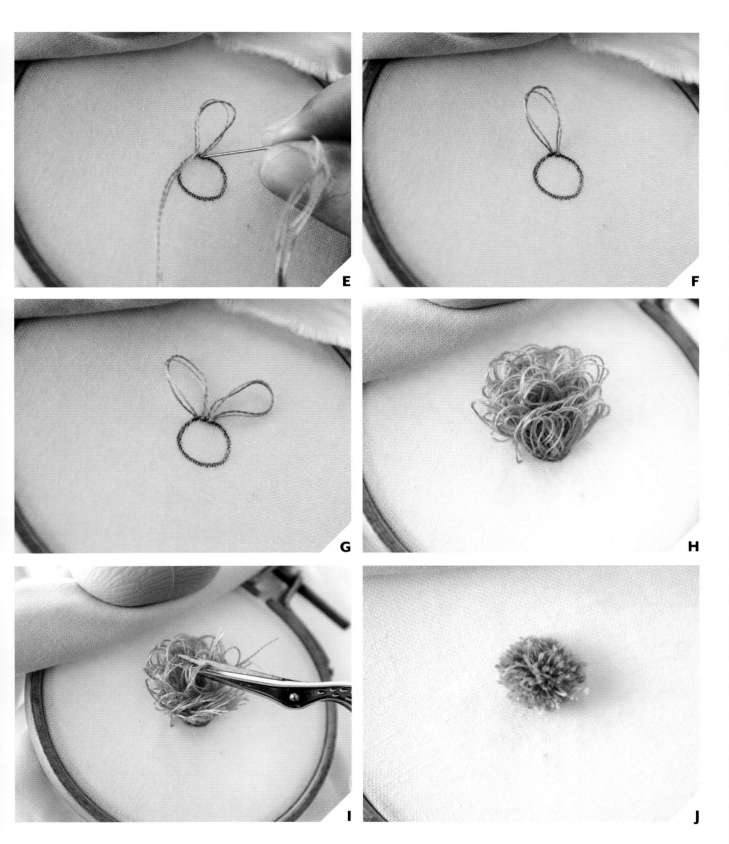

Couching Stitch

In this book, couching stitches are used to secure wire slips and felt padding to a base fabric. See Stumpwork Embroidery (page 46) to learn how to couching stitch a wire slip in place.

1. Place the felt piece onto the base fabric. Bring the needle up through the fabric and felt layers, about 5mm from the edge of the felt piece. **A**

2. Bring the needle down directly outside the edge of the felt piece through only the fabric layer. Pull the thread through, creating a straight stitch. **B**

3. Repeat Steps 1 and 2 around the edge of the felt piece until it is anchored in place. The stitches should be about 5mm apart. **C**

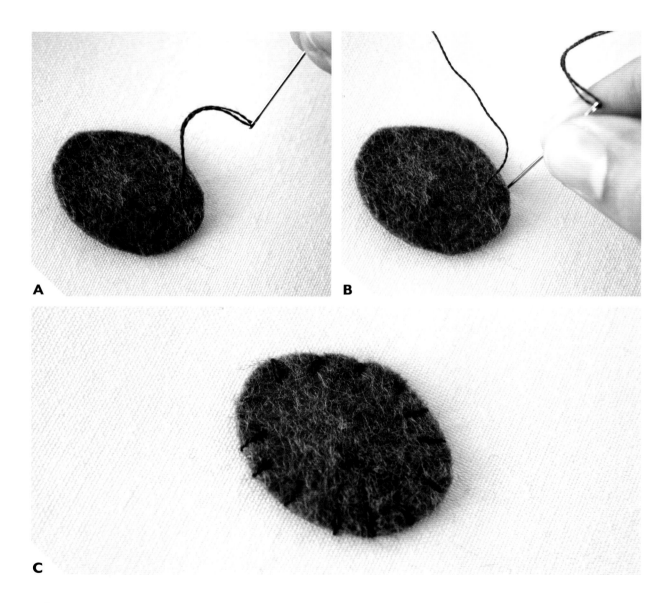

A

B

C

Long-and-Short Stitch

Long-and-short stitches are the foundation of thread painting. You can smoothly blend different thread colors by embroidering rows of stitches of varying lengths. This tutorial models how to blend four colors together, but an area can also be filled with long-and-short stitches of just one color. Keep stitches ¾" (1.9cm) or shorter.

1. Begin at one end of the area to be filled. I usually begin with the darkest shade in the gradient. Create a row of neatly aligned stitches that alternate between long and short. **A**

2. Embroider a second row of alternating long-and-short stitches in the second color. Fill in the gaps left by the short stitches of the first row. **B**

3. Blend a third row of long-and-short stitches into the second row with the third color. **C**

4. Finish filling in the area with a final row of long-and-short stitches in the fourth color. The stitches in this final row are different lengths, but they all end at the same line. **D**

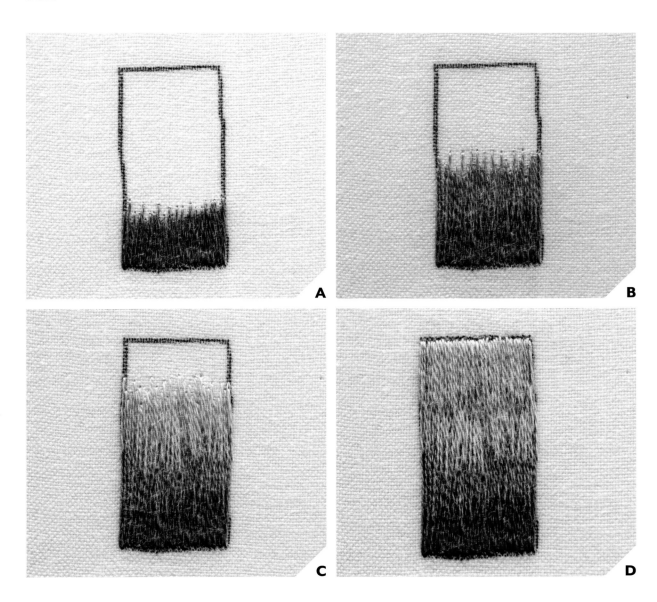

Thread Painting

I was drawn to this style of embroidery for its ability to capture the beauty of nature's smallest details with needle and thread. For me, thread painting is a way of honoring the embroidered subject. Your understanding and appreciation of your subject will grow stitch by stitch, and your patience will be rewarded with a beautiful embroidery that you can display proudly.

Mallard Duckling

FINISHED PROJECT SIZE: 4˝ × 5˝ (10.2 × 12.7cm)

Mallard ducklings are one of my favorite birds to embroider. Their comically large feet and unruly feathers make them a charming subject that always gives me a smile. I enjoy capturing them in joyful and lifelike animation, as they paddle along and stir up bubbles.

They're also the perfect project for learning thread painting! Combine simple long-and-short stitches with padded stumpwork, where base layers of felt add subtle depth, to capture the essence of a subject in realistic detail. The finished duckling will seem ready to swim out from the hoop!

Materials

1 embroidery hoop, size 5˝ (12.7cm)

Size 10 embroidery needle

Sulky Stick 'n Stitch paper

Scissors

Mallard Duckling Pattern (page 157)

Nurge 5˝ (12.7cm) display hoop, optional (or other display hoop/frame)

Thread and Fabric

2 squares 9˝ × 9˝ (22.9 × 22.9cm) of Kona cotton in Everglade

12˝ × 18˝ (30.5 × 45.7cm) sheet of Benzie wool-blend felt in Ecru

DMC six-stranded cotton embroidery floss colors (1 skein of each) • *see swatches below*

STITCHES USED IN THIS PROJECT

Satin Stitch, page 31

Seed Stitch, page 29

Couching Stitch, page 34

Backstitch, page 29

Long-and-Short Stitch, page 35

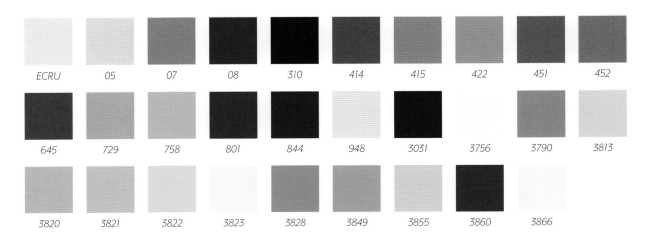

ECRU	05	07	08	310	414	415	422	451	452
645	729	758	801	844	948	3031	3756	3790	3813
3820	3821	3822	3823	3828	3849	3855	3860	3866	

Transfer the Pattern

See Transferring Patterns (page 27) for more information.

1. Print or draw the pattern onto the Sulky Stick 'n Stitch paper. Follow the printing instructions on the package.

2. Cut out the body and feet pieces from the transfer paper. Leave a ¼˝ (6mm) margin around each shape. Attach the stickers to the sheet of wool felt. **A**

3. Cut out each shape without margins. Remove the stickers so only the felt shapes remain. Keep track of the numbered shapes. **B**

Prepare the Padded Base

1. Thread a size 10 needle with one strand of DMC ECRU. Couching stitch the felt body outline #1 to the Kona Everglade fabric (secured in the hoop). **C**

2. Layer the felt body outline #2 over outline #1. Couching stitch the piece in place. **D**

3. Layer the felt body outline #3 over the other layers. Couching stitch the piece in place. **E**

4. Couching stitch the wing piece to the center of the body. Couching stitch the smaller foot piece to the body.

Couching stitch the larger foot piece on top of the smaller foot piece. **F**

5. Peel away the back of the sticker paper and adhere the pattern to the base fabric. Align the pattern with the padded felt outline. **G**

6. Layer a second piece of Kona Everglade behind the fabric with the felt body and pattern. Secure both layers in the 5˝ (12.7cm) hoop and tighten the hardware until the fabric is drum-tight. **H**

> **· LAYERING FABRIC ·**
> *There are multiple benefits to using two layers of fabric when embroidering. Many fabrics, even high-quality quilting cottons, are semitransparent. So, a second layer creates a fully opaque background, hiding the reverse side of your embroidery so it does not distract from the front. It also deepens the fabric to its full rich color. Additionally, a second layer of fabric provides better fabric tension by filling in the gap more completely between the inner and outer embroidery hoops.*

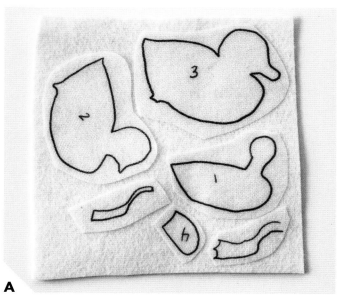

A

B

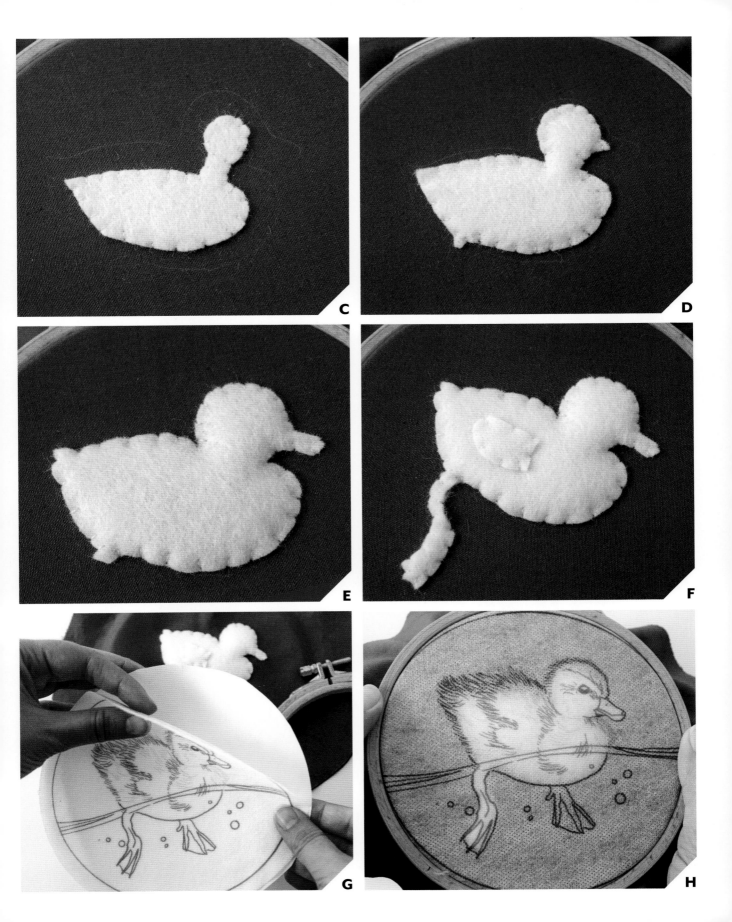

C

D

E

F

G

H

Embroider the Head

This pattern is stitched with one strand of DMC embroidery floss and a size 10 embroidery needle.

Eye

1. Make long-and-short stitches with DMC 310 to fill in the eye shape. Start at the inner corner of the eye, closest to the beak, and follow the curve of the eye. Add a reflection at the top of the eye with seed stitches of DMC 415 over the long-and-short stitches of DMC 310. **A**

2. Outline the eye with a backstitch of DMC 414. Add a few small straight stitches of DMC 3866 to the inner and outer corners of the eye. **B**

3. Blend DMC 3860, 07, 05, and 948 with long-and-short stitches to fill in the top of the beak, moving from dark to light as you stitch away from the face. Leave a gap for the nostril, as shown. **C**

4. Fill in the tip of the beak with long-and-short stitches of DMC 758. Then, embroider the underside of the beak with long-and-short stitches of DMC 3855 and DMC 758. Stitch the nostril with 2 small seed stitches of DMC 3860 and outline it with a backstitch of DMC 3855. **D**

5. Add a highlight to the end of the beak with two seed stitches in DMC 3866. **E**

6. Embroider long-and-short stitches of DMC 3031 in a stripe around the eye and along the stripe above the eye. Gently angle the stitches to show the curve of the head and give the illusion of feathers. **F**

7. Fill in the top of the head above the stripe with long-and-short stitches of DMC 08, 3790, and 3828. Vary the length of the stitches along the edge. Use 3828 mostly near the back and top of the head. **G**

8. Embroider the yellow feathers of the duckling's head with long-and-short stitches of DMC 3820 and 3821 blended together throughout. Use both colors through all the remaining space on the head. Then, blend long-and-short stitches of DMC 729 along the neckline and below the beak. **H**

9. Add straight stitches of DMC 3823 along the back of the head to look like wispy feathers. Angle the stitches and vary the length for a ruffled look. **I**

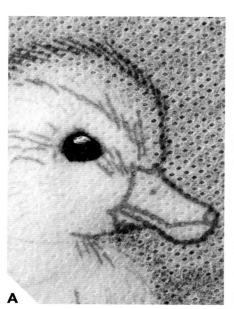

A

B

C

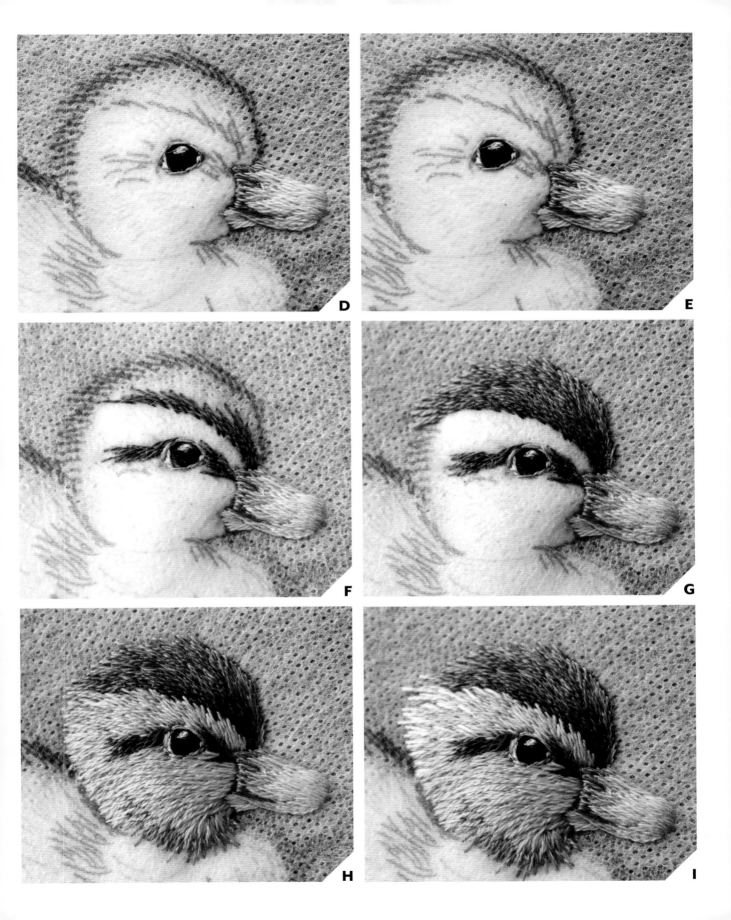

D

E

F

G

H

I

Embroider the Body

1. Embroider the two body stripes with long-and-short stitches of DMC 3031 and 801. **A**

· IMPERFECT STITCHES ·

A duckling's feathers are not perfectly preened. They are charmingly unruly and fluffy. Likewise, stitches should not be too perfectly blended in the body section of the pattern. Vary the angles of the stitches slightly, allowing them to overlap at times, to re-create the duckling's characteristically ruffled look.

2. Blend long-and-short stitches of DMC 3820 and 3821 into the neck and midsection. Gently curve the stitch direction in the area below the neck, following the pattern, to show the roundness of that section. **B**

3. Continue blending long-and-short stitches of DMC 3820 and 3821 to begin filling in the wing and tail feathers. **C**

4. Fill in the remaining area of the neck, wing, and tail feathers (above the waterline) with long-and-short stitches of DMC 3822. Add highlights to the tips of the tail feathers and wings with straight stitches of DMC 3823. **D**

5. Blend a gradient of DMC 422, 3828, 3790, and 08 with long-and-short stitches to fill in the duckling's lower abdomen as shown (below the waterline). DMC 08 should curve along the bottom of the duckling's body. **E**

· SHADOWS ·

The duckling's feathers are shadowed below the waterline. To create shadows in a thread-painted embroidery, choose two or three darker shades from the same color family as the primary thread colors. Blend a gradient that moves from lighter to darker hues to show how the light changes over the subject.

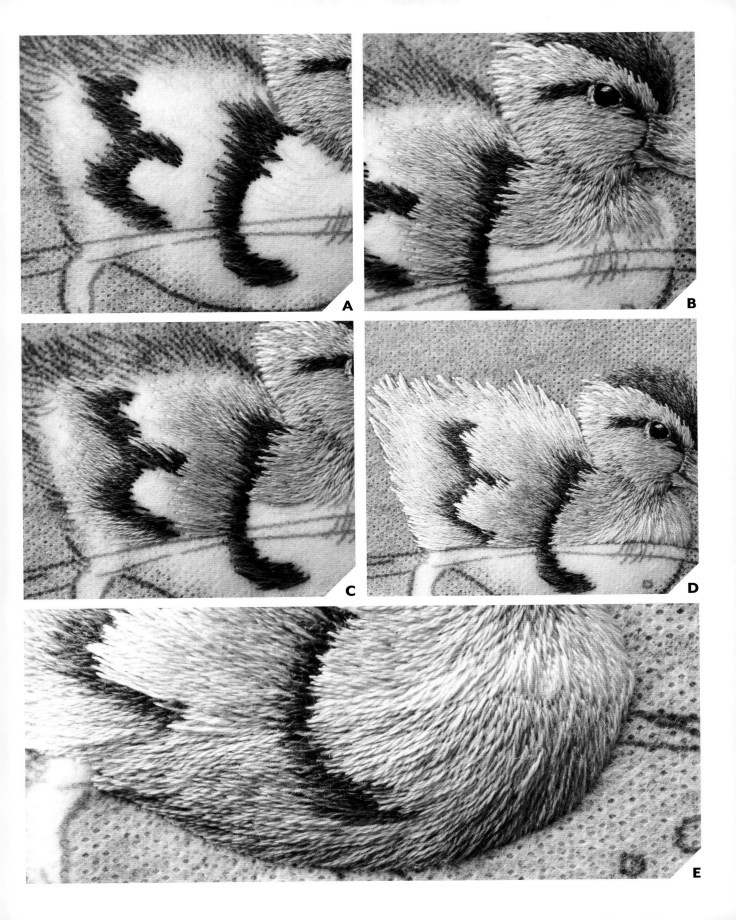

A

B

C

D

E

Embroider the Feet

1. Fill in the legs and toes with long-and-short stitches of DMC 844. Add highlights to the tops of the legs and toes with long-and-short stitches of DMC 645. Leave gaps between the toes. **A**

2. Blend DMC 451 and 452 with long-and-short stitches to fill in the webbing between the toes. Move from dark to light as you move away from the body. **B**

Embroider the Water

1. Embroider the waterline with long-and-short stitches of DMC 3756, 3813, and 3849, moving from light to dark from top to bottom. Make longer stitches than those used in the duckling's body. Overlap some stitches slightly so the waterline appears disturbed by the duckling's movement. Allow some stitches to spread over the duck's body. **C**

2. Remove the embroidery from the hoop and hand wash in warm, soapy water until the Sulky Stick 'n Stitch paper has washed away completely. Air-dry and then secure the embroidery back in the hoop.

3. Embroider bubbles of varied size below the waterline with Peking knots and French knots in DMC 3756. Some bubbles may overlap the duckling's feet and body. **D**

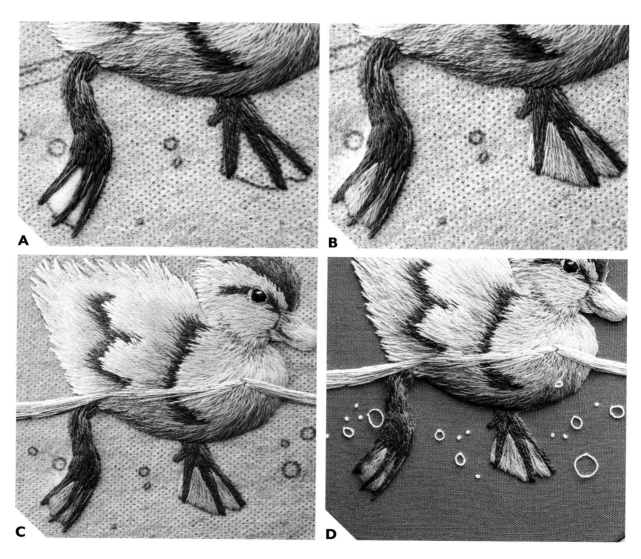

A

B

C

D

Finishing

See Displaying Embroidery (page 22) for instructions on how to secure your mallard duckling in a hoop or in a frame. I transferred mine to a 5˝ (12.7cm) Nurge display hoop.

Stumpwork Embroidery

The term stumpwork refers broadly to any three-dimensional embroidery. This style of embroidery encompasses a wide variety of techniques, including sewing raised stitches, embroidering over a padded surface, and using wire slips to create embroidered elements that can either stand alone or be attached to a flat surface. For an example using padded stumpwork, see Mallard Duckling Project (page 37).

Monarch Butterfly

FINISHED PROJECT SIZE: 2½˝ × 5˝ (6.4 × 12.7cm)

Monarch butterflies are well loved for their bold colors and the incredible migration they undertake each year across North America. This project shows you how to combine thread painting with wire-slip stumpwork embroidery to create a realistic monarch that looks ready to fly out of the hoop.

Materials

2 embroidery hoops, sizes 5˝ and 7˝

Size 10 embroidery needle

Tapestry or other large needle

Graphite paper for tracing

Jewelry wire, gauge 24

Wire cutters

Fabric glue

Craft-quality detail paintbrush

Small, pointed scissors

Beeswax thread conditioner

Monarch Butterfly Pattern (page 156)

Frame or display hoop, optional

Thread and Fabric

2 squares 9˝ × 9˝ (22.9 × 22.9cm) of Kona cotton in Spa Blue

10˝ × 10˝ (25.4 × 25.4cm) square of Kona cotton in Suede

DMC six-stranded cotton embroidery floss colors (1 skein of each) • *see swatches below*

STITCHES USED IN THIS PROJECT

Couching Stitch, page 34

Satin Stitch, page 31

Long-and-Short Stitch, page 35

Backstitch, page 29

Seed Stitch, page 29

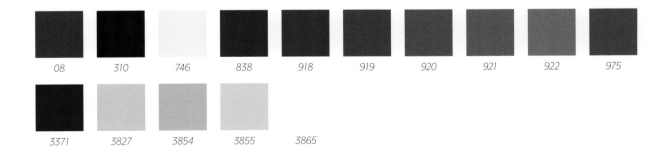

| 08 | 310 | 746 | 838 | 918 | 919 | 920 | 921 | 922 | 975 |

| 3371 | 3827 | 3854 | 3855 | 3865 |

Transfer the Pattern

See Transferring Patterns (page 27) for more information.

1. Transfer the body pattern to the Kona Spa Blue fabric. Layer a second piece of Kona Spa Blue fabric underneath and secure both layers together in the 5˝ hoop. **A**

2. Transfer the wing patterns to the Kona Suede fabric. Secure the fabric in the 7˝ hoop. **B**

Shape and Anchor the Wire

1. Cut a piece of wire long enough to go around the circumference of the wing, with about 3˝ (7.6cm) extra. Position the wire at the inner corner of the wing, with an extra 1½˝ (3.8cm) pointing toward where the butterfly's body will be and the rest of the extra wire pointing outward. **C**

2. Thread the size 10 embroidery needle with one strand of DMC 310. Bring the needle up through the fabric on one side of the wire. **D**

3. Bring the needle back down on the other side of the wire, directly across from where you came up, and pull the thread through to create a couching stitch that anchors the wire in place. **E**

4. Repeat, bending the wire to fit the wing shape and making spaced-apart couching stitches along the whole exterior of the wing to secure the wire to the fabric. Stop when you reach the inner corner again. You will have extra wire. **F**

5. Hold the two ends of wire at the inner corner and gently twist them together. If they are long enough, fold the twisted ends back toward the edge of the hoop to keep them out of the way while you embroider. **G**

6. Repeat Steps 1–5 to create wire slips for the other forewing and both hindwings.

Wrap the Wire

1. Completely wrap the exposed wire with couching stitches. Work slowly around the wing until the entire wire is covered, up to where the ends are twisted together. Keep the stitches uniform and as close to the wire as possible. **H**

> **· USING THREAD CONDITIONER ·**
> *Wrapping the wire can often cause the thread to fray. I recommend using a beeswax thread conditioner for this step. Simply run the length of the thread across the beeswax conditioner three times before threading the needle. It keeps the thread smooth and strengthens it, making it less likely to break or fray.*

2. Wrap the remaining three wing wires with couching stitches, following the same method. **I**

When transferring the pattern, position the inner corners of each wing away from the center of the hoop. This positioning keeps the loose ends of the wire slips out of your way while you are embroidering.

A

B

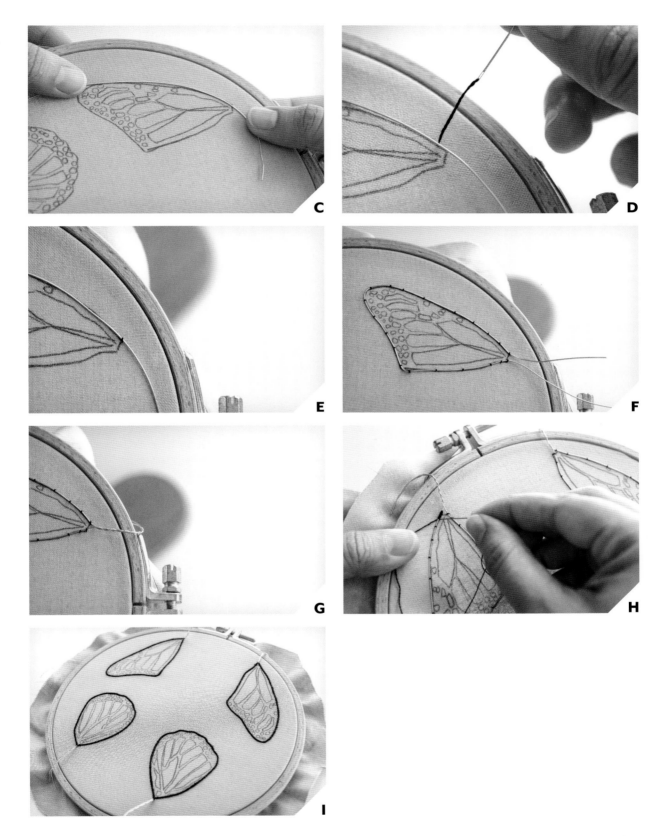

C

D

E

F

G

H

I

Embroider the Forewings

The monarch is embroidered with one strand of DMC embroidery floss and a size 10 embroidery needle. The stitch direction starts at the inner corner and follows the curve of the wing. When creating a gradient within each wing section, the darker colors should be closer to the corner of the wing.

1. Satin stitch the small spots along the outermost edge of the wing with DMC 3865. **A**

2. Satin stitch the larger outer spots with DMC 746 and the second row of spots with DMC 3827. **B**

3. Fill in the largest sections with a gradient of DMC 975, 918, 919, 920, and 921, blending the colors together with long-and-short stitches. **C**

4. Blend DMC 921, 922, and 3854 with long-and-short stitches to fill in the middle sections. **D**

5. Fill in the four smaller sections with long-and-short stitches of DMC 919 and 918 and DMC 921 and 922, as shown. **E**

6. Fill in the background of the wing with long-and-short stitches of DMC 310. Add small, straight stitches of DMC 3371 throughout the background, especially around the edges of each section, to create a softer and more natural look. Repeat Steps 1–6 for the other forewing. **F**

Embroider the Hindwings

The stitch direction of the hindwings starts at the inner corner and follows the curve of the wing. The gradients for the hindwing sections run in reverse when compared to the forewings, with the lightest colors positioned closer to the inner corner of the wing.

1. Satin stitch the spots along the edge of the wing with DMC 3865 and 3827. **G**

2. Fill in the five sections closest to the inner corner of the wing with long-and-short stitches made with a gradient of DMC 3855, 3854, and 922. **H**

3. Fill in the remaining sections with long-and-short stitches of DMC 3854, 922, 921, and 920. **I**

4. Fill in the background of the wing with long-and-short stitches of DMC 310. Add small, straight stitches of DMC 3371 throughout the background. Repeat Steps 1–4 for the other hindwing. **J**

A

B

Embroider the Body

Eyes and Antennae

1. Backstitch the antennae with DMC 310.

2. Satin stitch the eyes with DMC 310 and seed stitch a reflection detail in each eye with DMC 08. **A**

Abdomen

1. Stitch three rows of long-and-short stitches with DMC 3371 at the bottom of the abdomen. **B**

2. Fill in the rest of the abdomen and head with long-and-short stitches of DMC 838. Add markings (as shown) on the abdomen with straight stitches of DMC 3865. **C**

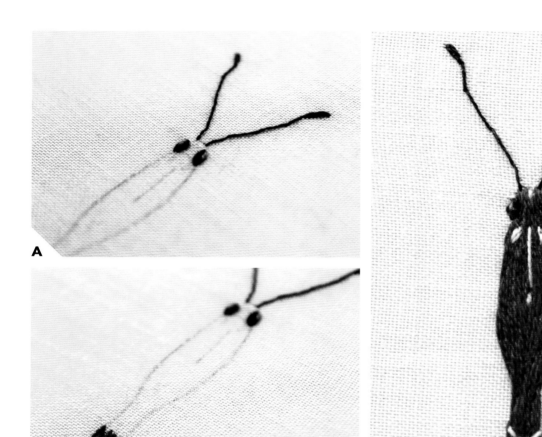

A

B

C

Assembly

Cut the Wings

1. Cut the wings apart from each other, leaving wide margins. **D**

2. With small, pointed scissors, carefully trim away the excess fabric around each wing. You can cut right up to the edge of the wing without cutting into the stitched edge. Trim away any excess threads on the back. **E–F**

Glue the Wings

1. Lightly paint the backside of each wing with fabric glue. **G**

2. Lightly apply glue to the wrapped wire edges of each wing as well. **H**

3. Wash the paintbrush to preserve it for future use. Allow the wings to dry completely before attaching them to the monarch's body.

D

E

F

G

H

Pour a small amount of glue into a container so that you can easily control the quantity that you apply to each wing. You do not want to oversaturate the wings with glue.

Attach the Wings

1. Refer to the pattern to mark the four spots where the wings attach to the body with a pencil or air-soluble marker. Use a tapestry needle to create holes at the marked spots through both layers of fabric. **A**

2. Pass the twisted wire of each wing through the hole until the wire is no longer visible and the corner of the wing appears to be attached to the base of the body. You may need to adjust the placement of the hole to avoid any gap between the body and the wing. Add all four wings. **B**

3. On the backside, gently twist each pair of wires together (right wings together and left wings together). Then, twist both sets of coupled wires together and fold them down along the length of the body. You can trim the excess wire if it is longer than the length of the abdomen. **C–D**

4. Add three couching stitches of DMC 838 to the inner corner of each wing, where the wire meets the fabric, to secure it in place. **E**

5. Gently adjust the wings to your preferred position. **F**

> **· POSITIONING THE WINGS ·**
>
> *I always position the forewings horizontally or downward to make the butterfly appear alive. Although butterfly wings are often depicted pointing upright in art, this position does not occur naturally with monarchs and many other butterfly species.*

Finishing

See Displaying Embroidery (page 22) for instructions on how to secure your monarch in a hoop or in a frame.

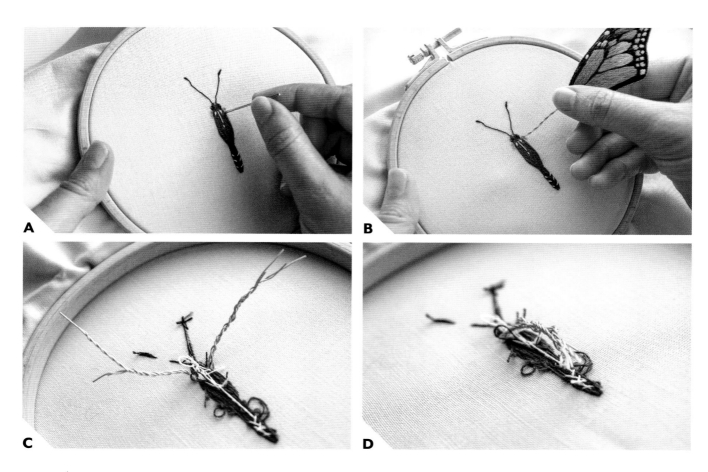

A

B

C

D

E

F

Miniature Thread Painting

Thread painting miniature designs is one of my favorite techniques. These tiny works of art are a great way to minimize waste by using leftover thread from larger projects. Half the fun of designing new miniature patterns with leftover threads is exploring how nature often uses the same palette across a variety of animal and plant life. In fact, I used leftover threads from the Mallard Duckling Project to create the charming Chipmunk Pendant Project in this chapter.

Smaller projects are also less time-consuming and allow you the satisfaction of starting and finishing a project in an afternoon. If you find that larger projects wear on your patience, pick up a smaller one! You will build experience and stamina, and then larger projects will no longer seem daunting or out of reach.

Miniature thread paintings are versatile in ways that larger embroideries are not. They can be finished as pieces of wearable art in jewelry settings or stitched onto clothes and accessories, such as bags or hats. They can also be made into bookmarks or keychains or framed as tiny decor pieces.

Chipmunk Pendant

FINISHED PROJECT SIZE: 1˝ × 1½˝ (2.5 × 3.8cm)

Learn firsthand why I adore miniature thread painting by stitching this comical little chipmunk with its treasured peanut and fluffy tail. I hope this piece brings you as much joy as it does me!

Materials

1 embroidery hoop, size 4˝ (10.2cm)

Size 9 and 10 embroidery needles

Graphite transfer paper

Scissors

Chipmunk Pattern (page 156)

Pendant setting (I am using a 1⅝˝ × 2⅛˝ or 42 × 55mm walnut setting from artbase on Etsy)

Necklace chain

Thread and Fabric

Gütermann cotton sewing thread in black

7˝ × 7˝ (17.8 × 17.8cm) square of Kona cotton in Seafoam

DMC six-stranded cotton embroidery floss (1 skein of each) • *see swatches below*

STITCHES USED IN THIS PROJECT

Satin Stitch, page 31

Seed stitch, page 29

Long-and-Short Stitch, page 35

Turkey Stitch, page 32

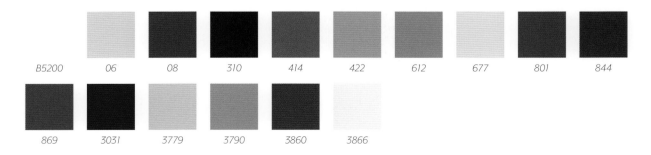

| B5200 | 06 | 08 | 310 | 414 | 422 | 612 | 677 | 801 | 844 |

| 869 | 3031 | 3779 | 3790 | 3860 | 3866 |

Transfer the Pattern

See Transferring Patterns (page 27) for more information.

1. Transfer the Chipmunk Pattern onto a piece of Kona Seafoam, using your preferred method. I used graphite paper. **A**

> **· LAYERING FABRIC FOR JEWELRY SETTINGS ·**
> *Use only one layer of fabric when embroidering patterns for jewelry or other miniature settings. Jewelry settings have very limited space, and their inserts or bezels are made to be very fitted. Wrapping two layers of fabric around an insert often creates unwanted bulk or untidiness.*

Embroider the Head

This pattern is stitched with one strand of embroidery floss and a size 10 needle unless otherwise specified.

> **· STITCH LENGTH ·**
> *Scale your stitches appropriately for the size of the project. Keep your stitches small, 2–5mm at the longest, to mimic the chipmunk's short fur length.*

Eye

1. Fill in the eye with small horizontal straight stitches of DMC 310. Curve the stitches around the contour of the eye. Add a highlight to the eye with one seed stitch of DMC B5200. **B**

2. Add long-and-short stitches of DMC 3866 along the top and bottom edge of the eye. Add a seed stitch of DMC 414 to the inner and outer corners of the eye. **C**

A

Top of Head

1. Blend DMC 869 and 3866 in long-and-short stitches along the length of the nose and above the eye. **D**

2. Fill in the remaining area from the nose to the top of the head with long-and-short stitches of DMC 08. **E**

Cheeks

1. Create a row of long-and-short stitches of DMC 3790 below the eye. Gently curve the stitches downward to show the roundness of the cheeks. **F**

2. Blend DMC 612 and 3866 in long-and-short stitches to fill in the rest of the cheek. Satin stitch the other cheek with DMC 612. **G**

B

C

D

E

F

G

Ears

1. Embroider the skin on the inside of the ear with long-and-short stitches. Blend DMC 3779 and 3860 to create a gradient within the ear. Embroider the fur outside of the ear with long-and-short stitches of DMC 3790. **A**

2. Satin stitch the other ear with DMC 3790. Angle the stitches to meet at the tip of the ear. **B**

Embroider the Body

Arm

1. Fill in a row of long-and-short stitches of DMC 3031 in the area below the cheek to create shadow and depth. Continue the row of long-and-short stitches along the length of the arm. Fill in a second row with DMC 3031 and 08. **C**

Hands

1. Blend in long-and-short stitches of DMC 869 along the arm, ending where the hands begin. Embroider the fingers of each hand with small, straight stitches of DMC 3779. Each finger requires only 1–2 stitches. **D**

A

B

C

D

Peanut and Nose

1. Embroider the nose with 2–3 straight stitches of DMC 844.

2. Embroider the peanut with long-and-short stitches of DMC 677. Fill in the entire area, including the gaps between the fingers on the chipmunk's left hand. **E**

> **· DOWNSCALED COLOR PALETTE ·**
>
> *We're using only one color to embroider the peanut, even though peanuts are textured and varied in color in real life. The peanut is a very small section of an already small pattern, so the stitches themselves add enough texture and depth to the area. Using more than one color in such a small area would be visually confusing or overwhelming. Downscale the color palette when planning a miniature embroidery and rely on your stitches to create dimension.*

Legs

1. Fill in the top section of the chipmunk's right leg with long-and-short stitches of DMC 612, 3790, and 869. **F**

2. Blend DMC 801 and 869 in long-and-short stitches to fill in the bottom of the right leg. **G**

3. Embroider long-and-short stitches of DMC 422 along the edge of the leg. Angle the stitches slightly downward to create a ruffled look. Fill in the fur of the chipmunk's inner leg with long-and-short stitches of DMC 06 and 3866. Vary the length of the stitches along the edge of the leg to make the fur appear fluffy. **H**

E

F

G

H

Stripes

1. Follow the stitch direction of the leg to fill in the stripes along the chipmunk's back with long-and-short stitches. Fill in the two outer stripes with DMC 844 and the middle stripe with DMC 3866. **A**

Whiskers

1. Thread a size 10 needle with one strand of Gütermann cotton sewing thread in black. Embroider the whiskers on both sides of the face with straight stitches. **B**

Tail

1. Thread a size 9 needle with one strand each of DMC 3031 and 844. Fill in the middle stripe of the tail with turkey stitches in these blended colors. Trim and fluff the threads. **C**

2. Thread a size 9 needle with one strand each of DMC 3790 and 869. Fill in the two outer stripes of the tail with turkey stitches in these blended colors. Trim and fluff the threads. **D**

> **· SEWING THREAD ·**
> *Add very fine details with cotton sewing thread in miniature and regular-sized thread-painted embroidery projects. Sewing thread is thinner than even one strand of regular cotton embroidery floss, so it is perfect for embroidering very delicate details, such as whiskers.*

A

B

C

D

Setting the Finished Embroidery

See Displaying Embroidery (page 22) for instructions on how to secure your chipmunk in a jewelry setting.

DECOR PROJECTS

Rosy Maple Moth

FINISHED PROJECT SIZE: 2½˝ × 4½˝ (6.4 × 11.4cm)

The rosy maple moth's bright colors and fluffy thorax make it a fun subject to embroider. I first spotted one of these cartoonishly adorable moths on my doorstep when returning home one evening, and it has remained one of my favorite moths to embroider ever since. Its vibrant pinks and sunny yellows will add a cheerful touch to your home.

Materials

2 embroidery hoops, sizes 5˝ (12.7cm) and 7˝ (17.8cm)

Sizes 9 and 10 embroidery needles

Tapestry or other large needle

Graphite paper

Jewelry wire, gauge 24

Wire cutters

Fabric glue

Craft-quality detail paintbrush

Small, pointed scissors

Beeswax thread conditioner

Rosy Maple Moth Pattern (page 159)

Frame, optional

Thread and Fabric

10˝ × 10˝ (25.4 × 25.4cm) square of Kona cotton in Peony

2 squares 9˝ × 9˝ (22.9 × 22.9cm) of Kona cotton in Aloha

12˝ × 18˝ (30.5 × 45.7cm) sheet of Benzie wool-blend felt in Ecru

DMC six-stranded cotton embroidery floss (1 skein of each):

STITCHES USED IN THIS PROJECT

Couching Stitch, page 34

Satin Stitch, page 31

Long-and-Short Stitch, page 35

Backstitch, page 29

Straight Stitch, page 29

Turkey Stitch, page 32

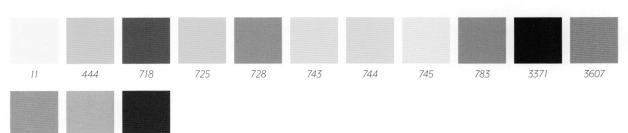

11   444   718   725   728   743   744   745   783   3371   3607

3608   3609   3803

Transfer the Pattern

See Transferring Patterns (page 27) for more information.

1. Transfer the body pattern to the Kona Aloha fabric. Layer a second piece of Kona Aloha fabric underneath and secure both layers together in the 5˝ (12.7cm) hoop. **A**

2. Transfer the wing patterns to the Kona Peony fabric. Secure the fabric in the 7˝ hoop. **B**

Prepare the Wire Slip

See Stumpwork Embroidery (page 46) for more information.

1. Couching stitch the forewing wire slips with DMC 744 and 3607 (alternating as shown) until they are wrapped completely. Twist the excess wire. **C**

2. Couching stitch the hindwing wire slips with DMC 3608 and 744 (alternating as shown) until wrapped completely. Twist the excess wire. **D**

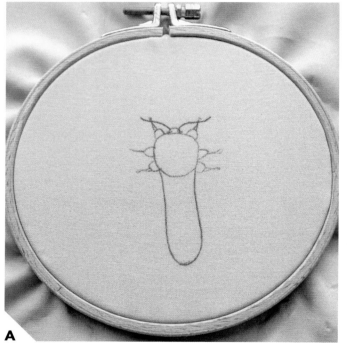

A

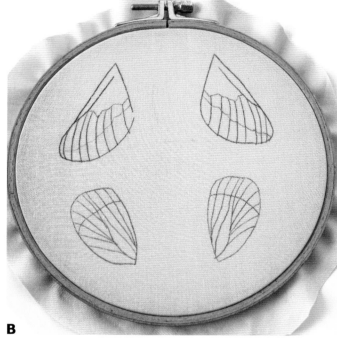

B

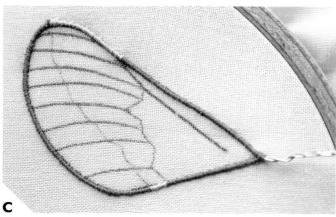

C

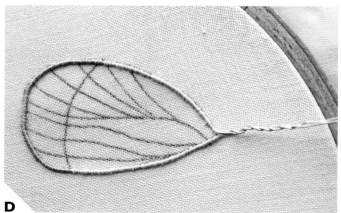

D

Embroider the Forewings

Each wing is stitched with one strand of DMC embroidery floss and a size 10 embroidery needle. The stitch direction starts at the inner corner and follows the curve of the wing.

1. Blend DMC 718 and 3607 in long-and-short stitches to fill in the inner corner of the wing. **A**

2. Fill in the middle section with a gradient of DMC 444, 743, and 744 in long-and-short stitches. Leave small gaps for the striped wing veins. **B**

3. Backstitch the veins in the middle section with DMC 11. Create a row of long-and-short stitches between the two stitched sections with DMC 3609. **C**

4. Fill in the final section with long-and-short stitches of DMC 3608 and 3607. Leave small gaps for the striped wing veins. **D**

5. Backstitch the veins in the final section with DMC 718. Create a row of long-and-short stitches of DMC 3803 between the middle and lower sections. Repeat Steps 1–5 to embroider the other forewing. **E**

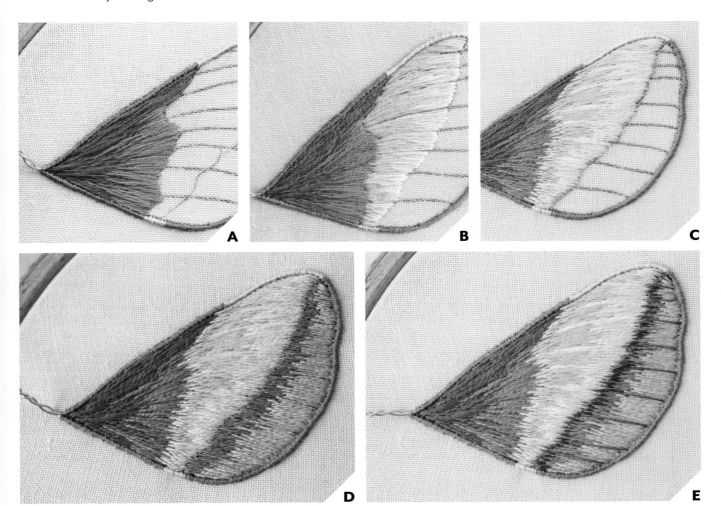

Embroider the Hindwings

The stitch direction starts at the inner corner and follows the curve of the wing.

1. Fill in the lower section with long-and-short stitches blending DMC 3608 and 3609. Straight stitch the veins with DMC 3607. **A**

2. Create a gradient with long-and-short stitches of DMC 444, 743, 744, and 745 in 3 of the inner sections (as shown). Leave small gaps for the wing veins. **B**

3. Fill in the remaining sections with long-and-short stitches of DMC 744 and 745. Leave small gaps for the wing veins. **C**

4. Backstitch the veins with DMC 725. Add a row of long-and-short stitches of DMC 3607 to blend the line between the yellow and pink sections. Repeat Steps 1–4 to embroider the other hindwing. **D**

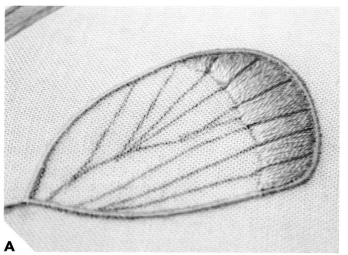

A

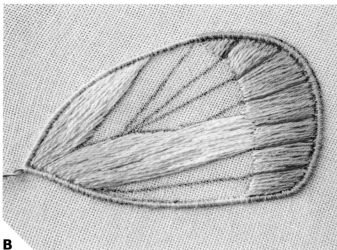

B

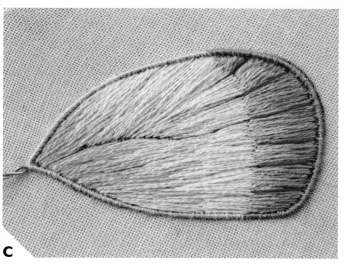

C

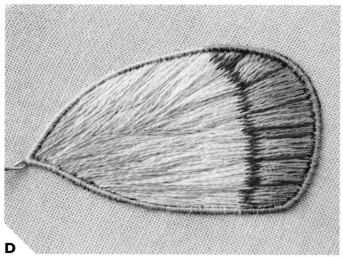

D

Embroider the Body

Pad the Thorax

1. Follow the pattern to cut two circles of the wool felt to pad the thorax.

2. Couching stitch the small felt circle to the fabric to create a raised thorax. Couching stitch the larger circle over the smaller circle. **A**

Legs, Eyes, and Antennae

1. Satin stitch and straight stitch the legs with DMC 718. **B**

2. Satin stitch the eyes with DMC 3371. Satin stitch the head with DMC 744. **C**

3. Backstitch the antennae with DMC 744 and add straight stitches in a V-shape to each side of both antennae. **D**

Thorax and Abdomen

1. Fill in the abdomen with long-and-short stitches of DMC 744 and 745. **E**

2. Thread a size 9 needle with two strands of DMC 728 and one strand of DMC 783.

3. Turkey stitch the thorax with the blended threads. Trim the turkey stitches to create a rounded, fluffy thorax. **F**

Assembly

See Stumpwork Embroidery (page 46) for more information about cutting out, gluing, and attaching the wings to the body.

1. Cut away all excess fabric from the wings. Paint glue onto the backs and edges of the wings. Let the wings dry completely. **A**

> **· ATTACHING WINGS ·**
>
> *When creating stumpwork moths, I like to attach the hindwings first, as these lower wings are mostly covered up by the forewings. Butterflies, such as monarchs, have a more open wingspan, so in that case, I attach the forewings first.*

2. Refer to the pattern to mark with a pencil or air-soluble marker the four spots where the wings attach to the body. Use the tapestry needle to make a hole in each spot. Attach the hindwings to the body by guiding the wire through the holes. Couching stitch the base of each wing in place. **B**

3. Attach the forewings in the same way. Adjust all four wings to your preferred position. **C**

Finishing

See Displaying Embroidery (page 22) for instructions on how to secure your rosy maple moth in a hoop or in a frame. I transferred mine to a vintage frame.

A

B

C

Luna Moth

FINISHED PROJECT SIZE: 4˝ × 5˝ (10.2 × 12.7cm)

The luna moth is an almost otherworldly creature, with transparent wings that give it a striking, ethereal appearance unlike that of any other moth. Its blended green-blue color palette and elongated forewings make it a more challenging subject to capture with needle and thread, but with patience, you can create a beautiful luna moth that looks ready to fly off into the night.

Materials

2 embroidery hoops, sizes 4˝ (10.2cm) and 7˝ (17.8cm)

Size 10 embroidery needles

Tapestry or other large needle

Graphite paper

Jewelry wire, gauge 24

Wire cutters

Fabric glue

Craft-quality detail paintbrush

Small, pointed scissors

Beeswax thread conditioner

Luna Moth Pattern (page 158)

Frame for display, optional

Thread and Fabric

10˝ × 10˝ (25.4 × 25.4cm) square of Kona cotton in Summer Pear

2 squares 7˝ × 7˝ (17.8 × 17.8cm) of Kona cotton in Berry

12˝ × 18˝ (30.5 × 45.7cm) sheet of Benzie wool-blend felt in Ecru

DMC six-stranded cotton embroidery floss (1 skein of each):

STITCHES USED IN THIS PROJECT

Couching Stitch, page 34

Satin Stitch, page 31

Straight Stitch, page 29

Long-and-Short Stitch, page 35

Backstitch, page 29

Turkey Stitch, page 32

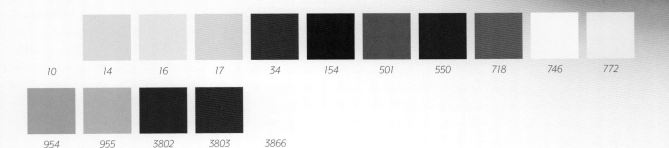

| 10 | 14 | 16 | 17 | 34 | 154 | 501 | 550 | 718 | 746 | 772 |

| 954 | 955 | 3802 | 3803 | 3866 |

Transfer the Pattern

See Transferring Patterns (page 27) for more information.

1. Transfer the body pattern to the Kona Berry fabric. Layer a second piece of Kona Berry fabric underneath and secure both layers together in the 5˝ (12.7cm) hoop. **A**

2. Refer to the pattern to cut two circles from the Benzie wool felt. Set aside for later.

3. Transfer the wing patterns to the Kona Summer Pear fabric. Secure the fabric in the 7˝ (17.8cm) hoop. **B**

Prepare the Wire Slip

See Stumpwork Embroidery (page 46) for more information.

1. Couching stitch the forewing wire slips. Use DMC 3802 at the top, 17 at the corner, 718 at the underside, and 10 on the inside edge, as shown, until they are wrapped completely. Twist the wire ends. **C**

2. Couching stitch the hindwing wire slips. Use DMC 772 at the top, 10 along the long edge and tail of the wing, and 718 on the curved underside, as shown, until they are wrapped completely. Twist the wire ends. **D**

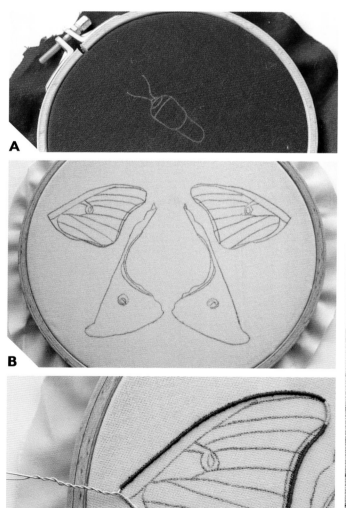

A

B

C

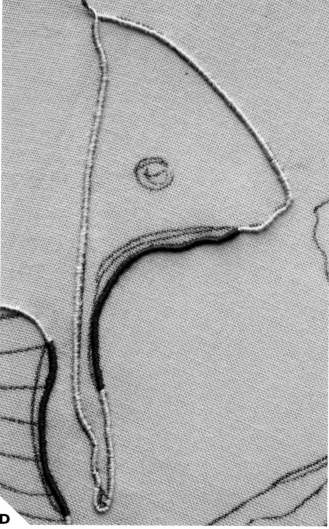

D

Embroider the Forewings

Each wing is stitched with one strand of DMC embroidery floss and a size 10 embroidery needle. The stitch direction for the forewing starts at the inner corner and follows the curve of the wing.

1. Fill in the top section of the wing with long-and-short stitches of DMC 3803 and 3802. **A**

2. Embroider the eyespot with long-and-short stitches of DMC 3802, 718, and 17, as shown. Satin stitch the center of each eyespot with DMC 3866. Blend DMC 34 throughout the top section. Outline the top section, including the eyespot, with backstitches of DMC 550. **B**

3. Fill in the corner and bottom edge section of the wing with long-and-short stitches of DMC 746. **C**

4. Fill in the main wing sections with a gradient of long-and-short stitches of DMC 954, 955, 16, and 14. Leave small gaps for the wing section outlines. **D**

5. Fill in the wing section under the eyespot with a gradient of long-and-short stitches of DMC 501, 954, and 955. **E**

6. Backstitch the wing sections with DMC 746. **F**

7. Fill in the curved bottom edge of the wing with a row of long-and-short stitches of DMC 718. Fill in the corner edge with long-and-short stitches of DMC 17. Repeat Steps 1–7 to embroider the second forewing. **G**

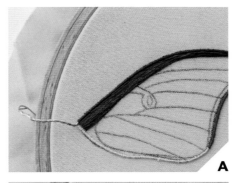
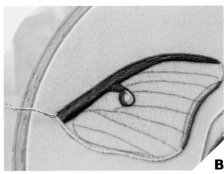
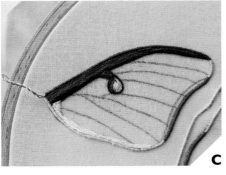
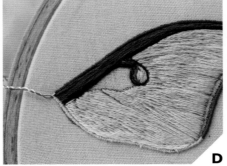
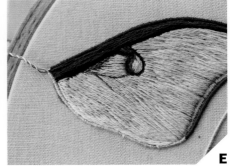
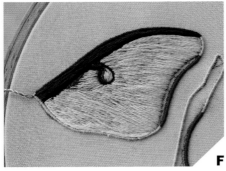
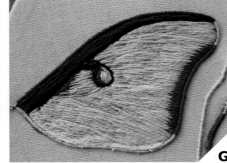

Embroider the Hindwings

The stitch direction for the hindwings starts at the inner corner and follows the curve of the wing.

1. Satin stitch the center of the eyespot with DMC 3866 and 718. Fill in the area around it with long-and-short stitches of DMC 17. Backstitch an outline around the eyespot with DMC 550. **A**

2. Blend a gradient of long-and-short stitches of DMC 954, 955, 16, and 14 to fill in the main body of the hindwing. **B**

3. Continue to blend long-and-short stitches of DMC 954, 955, 16, and 14 downward into the tail of the hindwing. **C**

4. Blend long-and-short stitches of DMC 746 and 718 along the curved edge of the wing, from the body of the wing to the tail. Repeat Steps 1–4 to embroider the second hindwing. **D**

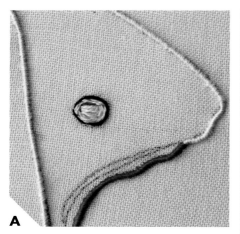

A

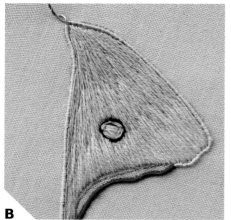

B

C

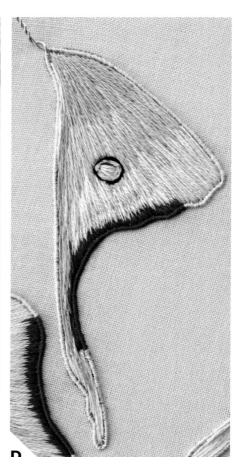

D

Embroider the Body

1. Satin stitch the top of the head with DMC 34 and 746. Long-and-short stitch the top section of the body with DMC 34, 3803, and 154. **A**

2. Couching stitch the two circles of felt to the fabric on top of one another to form the padded thorax. **B**

3. Turkey stitch the thorax with DMC 746. Trim to create a fuzzy, rounded thorax. Long-and-short stitch the remainder of the abdomen with DMC 746. **C**

4. Backstitch the long lines of the antennae with DMC 17. Add straight stitches in the same color in a V-shape along both sides of each antenna. **D**

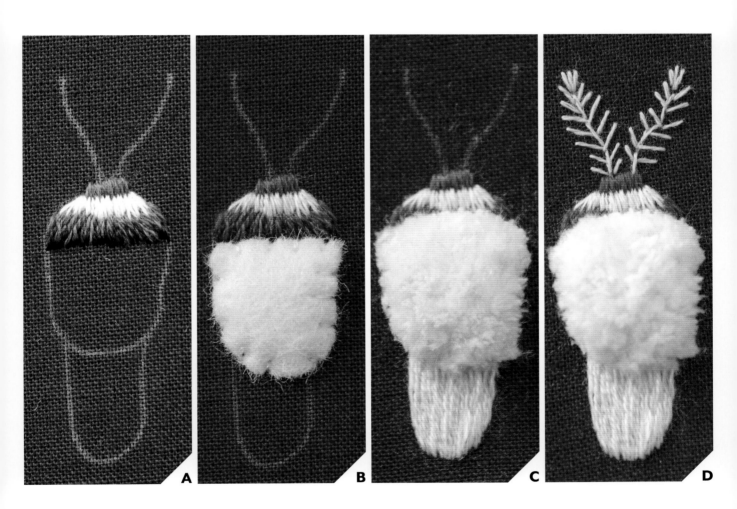

A   B   C   D

Assembly

See Stumpwork Embroidery (page 46) for more information about cutting out, gluing, and attaching the wings to the body.

1. Cut away all excess fabric from the wings. Paint glue onto the backs and edges of the wings. Let the wings dry completely.

2. Refer to the pattern to mark with a pencil or air-soluble marker the 4 spots where the wings attach to the body. Use the tapestry needle to make a hole in each spot. Attach the hindwings to the body by guiding the wire through the holes. Couching stitch the base of each wing in place.

3. Attach the forewings in the same way. Adjust all four wings to your preferred position.

Finishing

See Displaying Embroidery (page 22) for instructions on how to secure your luna moth in a hoop or in a frame. I transferred mine to an oval 4˝ × 6˝ (10.2 × 15.2cm) vintage frame.

White-Tailed Bumblebee

FINISHED PROJECT SIZE: 2˝ × 2¾˝ (5.1 × 7cm)

The gentle bumblebee is an important pollinator, well loved by gardeners and nature enthusiasts alike. Capture its smallest details with thread painting, its fuzzy texture with turkey stitches, and its animated wings with wire-slip stumpwork. The finished bumblebee may be small in size, but it captivates and awes in a big way.

Materials

2 embroidery hoops, sizes 4˝ (10.2cm) and 5˝ (12.7cm)

Sizes 9 and 10 embroidery needles

Tapestry or other large needle

Graphite paper

Jewelry wire, gauge 24

Wire cutters

Fabric glue

Craft-quality detail paintbrush

Small, pointed scissors

Beeswax thread conditioner

White-Tailed Bumblebee Pattern (page 156)

4˝ × 3˝ (10.2 × 7.6cm) Nurge flexi hoop, optional

Thread and Fabric

2 squares 9˝ × 9˝ (22.9 × 22.9cm) of Kona cotton in Sky

7˝ × 7˝ (17.8 × 17.8cm) square of Kona cotton in White

DMC six-stranded cotton embroidery floss (1 skein of each):

STITCHES USED IN THIS PROJECT

Couching Stitch, page 34

Satin Stitch, page 31

Long-and-Short Stitch, page 35

Backstitch, page 29

Seed Stitch, page 29

Turkey Stitch, page 32

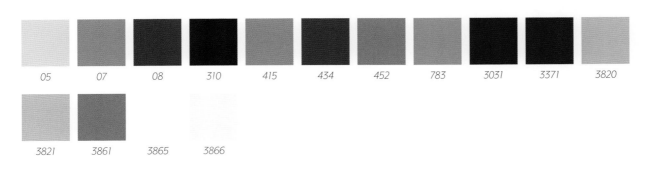

| 05 | 07 | 08 | 310 | 415 | 434 | 452 | 783 | 3031 | 3371 | 3820 |

| 3821 | 3861 | 3865 | 3866 |

Transfer the Pattern

See Transferring Patterns (page 27) for more information.

1. Transfer the body pattern to the Kona Sky fabric, using your preferred transfer method. Layer a second piece of Kona Sky fabric underneath and secure both layers together in the 5˝ (12.7cm) hoop. **A**

2. Transfer the wing patterns to the Kona White fabric. Secure the fabric in the 4˝ (10.2cm) hoop. **B**

Prepare the Wire Slip

See Stumpwork Embroidery (page 46) for more information.

1. Couching stitch the wing wire slips with DMC 3861 at the upper edge of each wing and DMC 452 on the remainder of the wing (as shown) until they are wrapped completely. **C**

Embroider the Wings

Unless otherwise specified, each section is stitched with one strand of DMC embroidery floss and a size 10 embroidery needle.

1. Backstitch the veins of each wing with DMC 07. **D**

2. Line the bottom edge of each wing with long-and-short stitches of DMC 452. **E**

3. Blend in long-and-short stitches of DMC 05. **F**

4. Fill in the remainder of the wing with long-and-short stitches of DMC 3866. **G**

5. Add straight stitches of DMC 3861 to the top edge of the wing and the two center veins. **H**

A

B

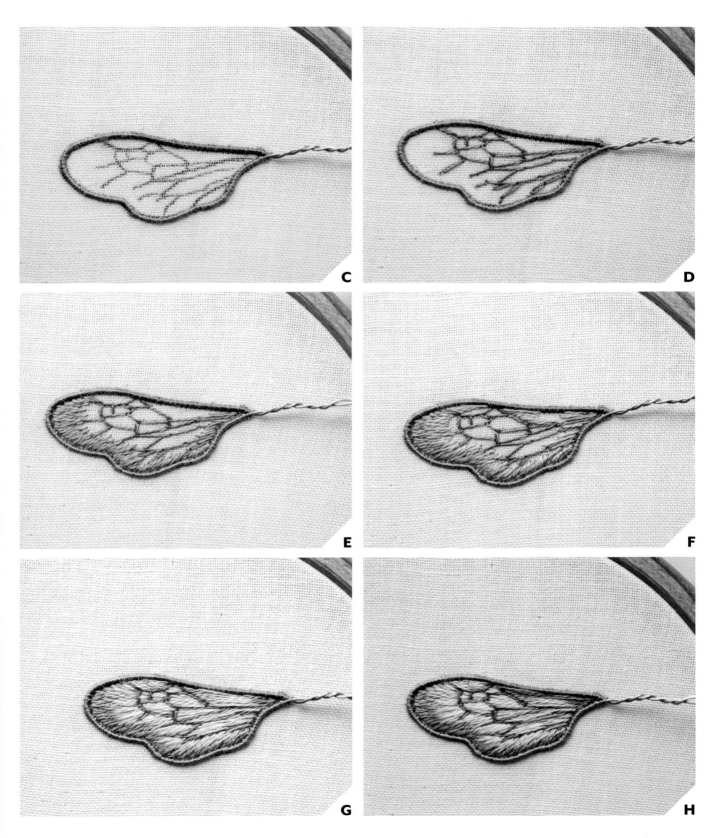

Abdomen

1. Fill in the dark stripes with long-and-short stitches of DMC 3371 and 3031. **A**

2. Create a gradient with long-and-short stitches of DMC 434, 783, 3820, and 3821 in the middle stripe. **B**

3. Blend DMC 3865 and 3866 in long-and-short stitches to fill in the bottom section. **C**

A

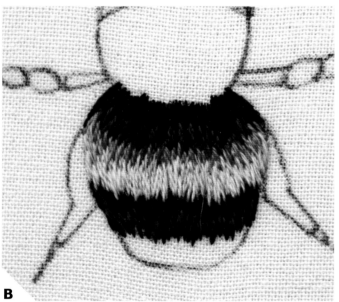

B

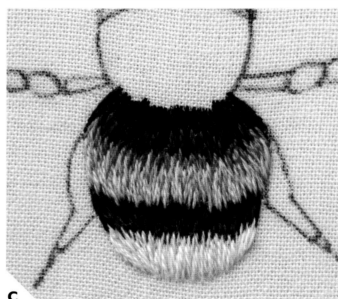

C

Thorax, Head, and Legs

1. Blend DMC 3031, 434, and 783 in long-and-short stitches to fill in the first two sections of the upper thorax. **A**

2. Satin stitch the eyes with DMC 310. Create a reflection in each eye by adding a seed stitch of DMC 415. Satin stitch the head with DMC 08. **B**

3. Blend DMC 3031 and 08 in long-and-short stitches to fill in the legs. Add straight stitches of DMC 3821 between the leg sections on the two front legs. **C**

4. Backstitch the two antennae with one strand of DMC 3371. **D**

5. Thread a size 9 needle with two strands of DMC 3371 and one strand of DMC 310.

6. Fill in the thorax with turkey stitches of the blended threads. Trim to create a fluffy thorax. **E**

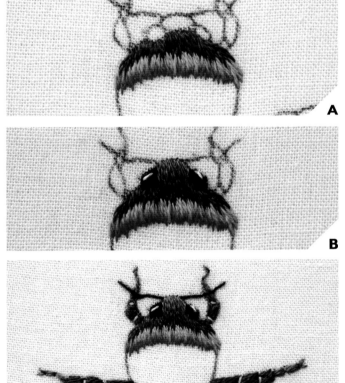

Assembly

See Stumpwork Embroidery (page 46) for more information about cutting out, gluing, and attaching the wings to the body.

1. Cut away all excess fabric from the wings. Paint glue onto the backs and edges of the wings. Let the wings dry completely.

2. Refer to the pattern to mark with a pencil or air-soluble marker the two spots where the wings attach to the body. Use the tapestry needle to make a hole in each spot. Attach the wings to the body by guiding the wire through the holes. Adjust the wings to your preferred position. Couching stitch the base of each wing in place.

Finishing

See Displaying Embroidery (page 22) for instructions on how to secure your white-tailed bumblebee in a hoop or in a frame. I transferred mine to a 4″ × 3″ (10.2 × 7.6cm) Nurge flexi hoop.

Bearded Iris

FINISHED PROJECT SIZE: 2½˝ × 6˝ (6.4 × 15.2cm)

Bearded irises, the colorful harbingers of spring, are one of my favorite flowers. With this pattern, you can embroider an iris that will bloom year-long in your home. Combine thread painting and wire-slip stumpwork to re-create these beautiful flowers. Learn how dimensional stitches, such as turkey stitches, can be worked on a wire slip to give the iris its iconic fuzzy beard and add extra texture and interest to the embroidery.

Materials

2 embroidery hoops, sizes 9˝ (22.9cm) and 4˝ (10.2cm)

Size 9 and 10 embroidery needles

Tapestry or other large needle

Graphite transfer paper

Jewelry wire, gauge 24

Wire cutters

Fabric glue

Craft-quality detail paintbrush

Small, pointed scissors

Beeswax thread conditioner

Bearded Iris Pattern (page 156)

Frame for display, optional

Thread and Fabric

2 squares 13˝ × 13˝ (33 × 33cm) of Kona cotton in Pesto

7˝ × 7˝ (17.8 × 17.8cm) square of Kona cotton in Petal Pink

DMC six-stranded cotton embroidery floss (1 skein of each):

STITCHES USED IN THIS PROJECT

Couching Stitch, page 34

Satin Stitch, page 31

Long-and-Short Stitch, page 35

Turkey Stitch, page 32

Seed Stitch, page 29

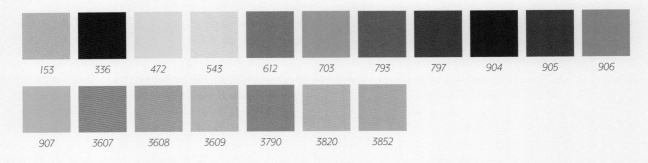

| 153 | 336 | 472 | 543 | 612 | 703 | 793 | 797 | 904 | 905 | 906 |

| 907 | 3607 | 3608 | 3609 | 3790 | 3820 | 3852 |

Transfer the Pattern

See Transferring Patterns (page 27).

1. Transfer the Bearded Iris Pattern to the Kona Pesto fabric, using your preferred transfer method. Layer a second piece of Kona Pesto fabric underneath and secure both layers together in the 9˝ (22.9cm) hoop. **A**

2. Transfer the petal pattern to the Kona Petal Pink fabric and secure the fabric in the 4˝ (10.2cm) hoop. **B**

Prepare the Wire Slip

See Stumpwork Embroidery (page 46) for more information.

1. Couching stitch the smallest petal with DMC 3609 until the wire is wrapped completely.

2. Couching stitch the larger petal with DMC 3820 and 336 (as shown) until the wire is wrapped completely. Twist both wires. **C**

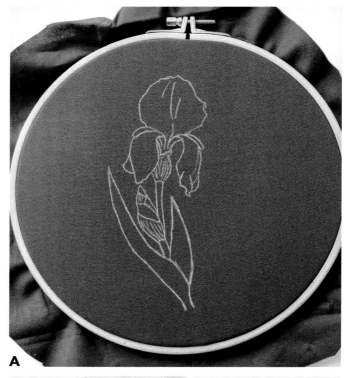

A

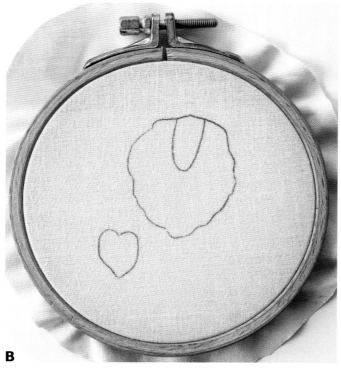

B

C

Embroider the Petals

This pattern is stitched with one strand of embroidery floss and a size 10 needle unless otherwise specified in the directions.

1. Begin at the narrowest part of the small petal. Blend DMC 3607 and 3609 in long-and-short stitches to fill in the petal. **A**

1. Blend DMC 336, 797, and 793 in long-and-short stitches to fill in the largest section of the larger petal. **B**

2. Thread the size 9 needle with one strand each of DMC 3820 and 3852. Fill in the bearded part of the petal with turkey stitches. Trim and fluff the threads to make a fuzzy beard. **C**

A

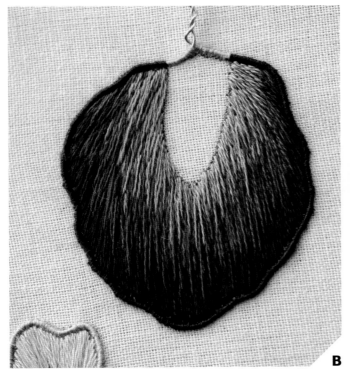

B

C

Embroider the Iris

Stem and Bud

1. Switch to the Kona Pesto hoop. Fill in the two stem sections with a gradient of long-and-short stitches of DMC 907, 703, and 906. **A**

2. Blend DMC 472, 907, and 906 in long-and-short stitches to fill in the base of the bud. Gently curve the stitches to show the roundness of the bud. **B**

3. Blend the line where the bud and the stem meet with long-and-short stitches of DMC 472.

4. Fill in the middle section of the bud with long-and-short stitches of DMC 543 and 612. **C**

5. Blend DMC 905, 906, 472, 3790, and 543 with long and short stitches to fill in the two remaining top sections. Angle the stitches in each section inward so the petals of the bud appear closed. **D**

6. Blend DMC 906, 472, 612, and 543 in long-and-short stitches to embroider the rounded base of the open iris. **E**

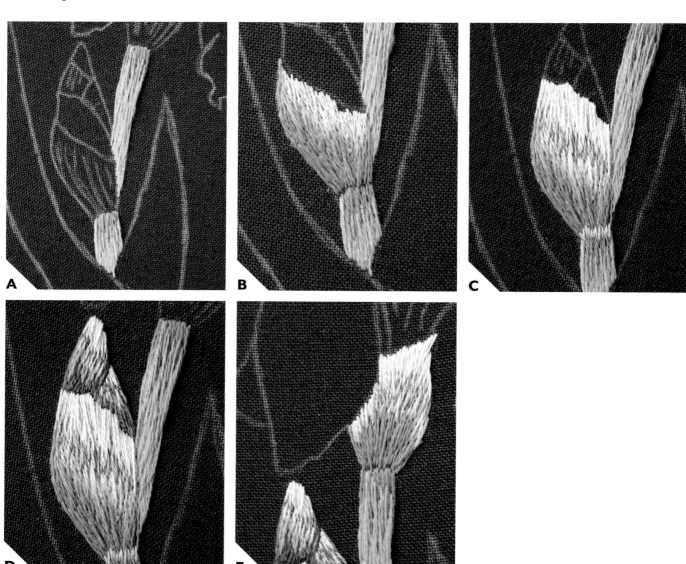

A

B

C

D

E

Leaves

1. Begin at the base of the longest leaf. Embroider long-and-short stitches of DMC 905 along the whole length of the leaf. Curve the stitches to follow the curve of the leaf. Make long-and-short stitches of DMC 906 at the tip of the leaf. **A**

2. Begin at the base of the smaller leaf. Blend DMC 907, 906, 905, and 904 in long-and-short stitches to fill in the leaf. **B**

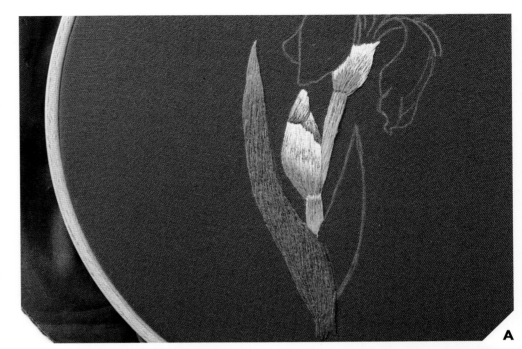

A

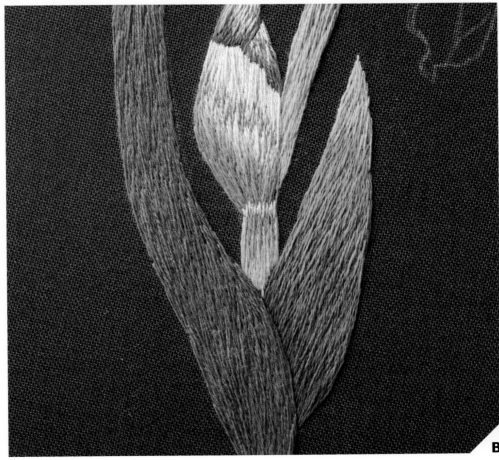

B

Flower

1. Blend DMC 472 and 907 in long-and-short stitches at the base of the three petals. **A**

2. Embroider the upright petal with long-and-short stitches. Blend DMC 3607, 3608, 3609, and 153 to create a gradient that begins at the bottom of the petal with the darkest color and radiates up and out to the end of the petal. **B**

3. Embroider the underside of the two lower petals with long-and-short stitches of DMC 336. **C**

4. Blend DMC 793, 797, and 336 in long-and-short stitches to fill in the right petal. Gently curve the stitches to follow the curve of the petal. **D**

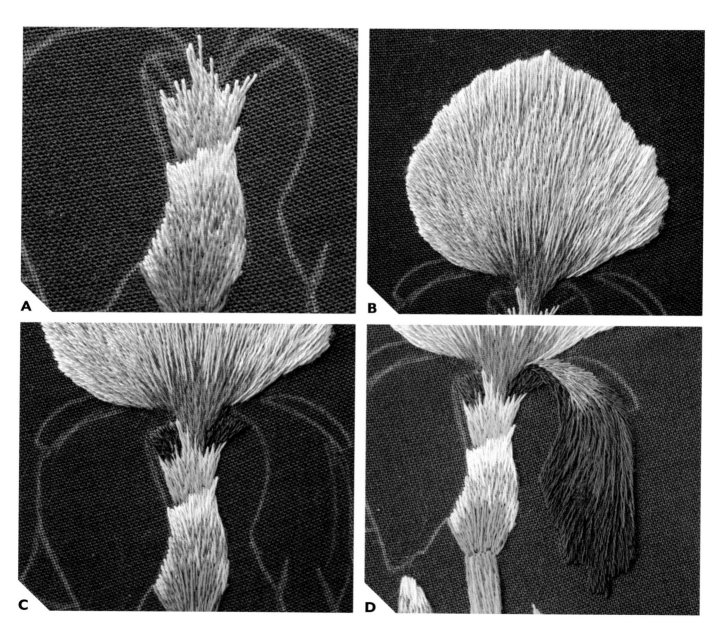

5. Blend DMC 793, 797, and 336 in long-and-short stitches to fill in the largest section of the left petal. Gently curve the stitches to follow the curve of the petal. **E**

6. Fill in the bottom smaller section of the left petal with long-and-short stitches of DMC 336. Angle the stitches toward the larger petal to create the appearance of a fold. **F**

7. Thread a needle with two strands of DMC 3820. Turkey stitch the beards of the two lower petals. Trim and fluff the threads. **G**

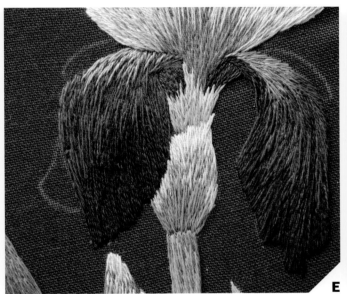

E

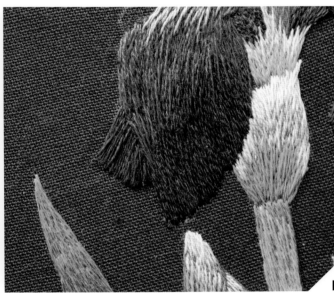

F

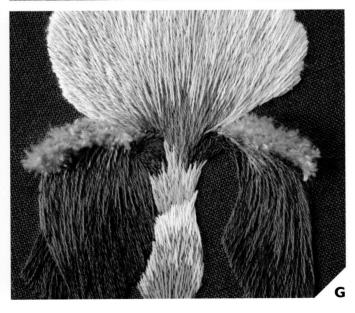

G

Assembly

See Stumpwork Embroidery (page 46) for more information about cutting out, gluing, and attaching the petals to the flower.

1. Cut away all excess fabric from the stumpwork petals. Paint glue onto the backs and edges of the petals. Let them dry completely.

2. Refer to the pattern to mark with a pencil or air-soluble marker the spots where the petals attach to the flower. Use the tapestry needle to make a hole in each spot. Attach the petals to the flower by guiding the wire through the holes. Adjust the petals to your preferred position. The small pink petal should stand upright above the large pink petal. The large bearded petal should extend in the opposite direction, standing over the stem. Couching stitch the base of each petal in place.

Finishing

See Displaying Embroidery (page 22) for instructions on how to secure the bearded iris in a hoop or in a frame. I transferred mine to a vintage frame.

Columbine Flower

FINISHED PROJECT SIZE: 2˝ × 4˝ (5.1 × 10.2cm)

Columbines are arresting and beautiful flowers, with pointed, star-shaped outer petals and soft, rounded inner petals. Although some flowers' petals are designed to attract select pollinators, columbines attract a wide variety of pollinators, including bees, moths, butterflies, and hummingbirds. Style the framed Columbine Flower embroidery with any of the pollinator decor pieces in this book for a striking display that captures the beauty of the pollinator-flower relationship.

Materials

2 embroidery hoops, sizes 7˝ (17.8cm) and 4˝ (10.2cm)

Size 9 and 10 embroidery needles

Tapestry or other large needle

Graphite transfer paper

Jewelry wire, gauge 24

Wire cutters

Fabric glue

Craft-quality detail paintbrush

Small, pointed scissors

Beeswax thread conditioner

Columbine Flower Pattern (page 156)

5.7˝ × 7.5˝ (14.5 × 19cm) Nurge oval flexi hoop, optional

Thread and Fabric

2 squares 10˝ × 10˝ (25.4 × 25.4cm) of Kona cotton in Dove

7˝ × 7˝ (17.8 × 17.8cm) square of Kona cotton in Petal Pink

12˝ × 18˝ (30.5 × 45.7cm) sheet of Benzie wool-blend felt in Fern

DMC six-stranded cotton embroidery floss (1 skein of each):

STITCHES USED IN THIS PROJECT

Couching Stitch, page 34

Long-and-Short Stitch, page 35

Backstitch, page 29

Turkey Stitch, page 32

| 18 | 151 | 818 | 904 | 905 | 906 | 907 | 3804 | 3805 | 3806 | 3820 |

Transfer the Pattern

See Transferring Patterns (page 27) for more information.

1. Cut the small circle from the pattern out of the Benzie felt.

2. Transfer the Columbine Flower Pattern to the Kona Dove fabric, using your preferred method. Layer a second piece of Kona Dove fabric underneath and secure both layers together in the 7˝ (17.8cm) hoop. **A**

3. Transfer the petal pattern shapes to the Kona Petal Pink fabric and secure the fabric in the 4˝ (10.2cm) hoop. **B**

Prepare the Wire Slip

See Stumpwork Embroidery (page 46) for more information.

1. Couching stitch each petal with DMC 818 until the wires are wrapped completely. Twist the ends of the wires. **C**

A

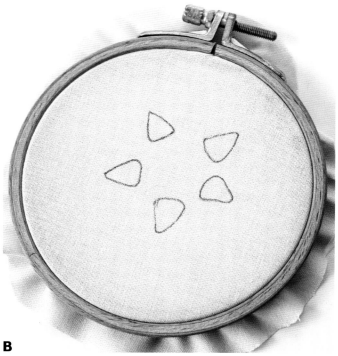

B

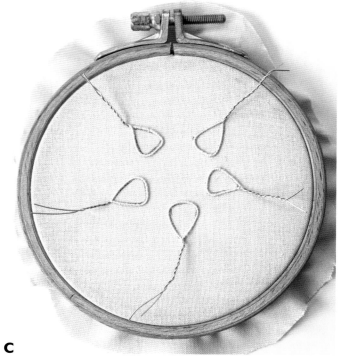

C

Embroider the Flower

This pattern is stitched with one strand of embroidery floss and a size 10 needle unless otherwise specified in the directions.

1. Blend DMC 3806, 151, and 818 in long-and-short stitches to fill in the small petals. Begin at the narrowest part of the petal and curve the stitches out toward the edges of the petal. **A**

2. Repeat Step 1 until all five petals are filled. **B**

3. Switch to the larger hoop. Blend DMC 3806, 3805, and 3804 in long-and-short stitches to fill in the larger petals on the Dove fabric. Gently curve the stitches to follow the shape of each petal up to a point. **C**

A

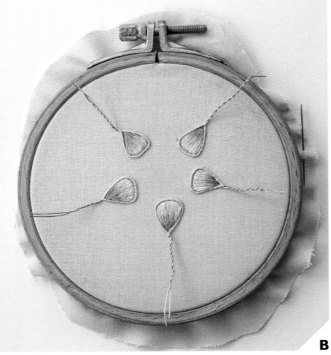

B

C

Leaves

1. Backstitch the veins of each leaf with DMC 904. **A**

2. The right leaf is split into three sections. Fill in the lower two sections first. Begin at the base of the leaf and blend DMC 907, 906, 905, and 904 outward in long-and-short stitches. **B**

3. Fill in the middle section of the right leaf with long-and-short stitches blending DMC 907, 906, 905, and 904. Create a border between the leaf sections by bringing the long-and-short stitches of DMC 907 down along the edges of the section. **C**

4. Blend DMC 907, 906, 905, and 904 in long-and-short stitches to fill in the two sections of the left leaf. **D**

A

B

C

D

Stem, Bud, and Center

1. Embroider each section of the stem with long-and-short stitches of DMC 904. **E**

2. Blend DMC 151, 3806, 907, and 906 in long-and-short stitches to fill in the shape of the bud. Stitch the small curly leaves at the base of the bud with straight stitches of DMC 907. **F**

3. Couching stitch the felt padding to the center of the flower. **G**

4. Thread the size 9 needle with one strand each of DMC 18 and 3820. Turkey stitch the flower center. Trim and fluff the threads to make a fluffy center. **H**

E

F

G

H

Assembly

See Stumpwork Embroidery (page 46) for more information about cutting out, gluing, and attaching the petals to the flower.

1. Cut away all excess fabric from the stumpwork petals. Paint glue onto the backs and edges of the petals. Let them dry completely. **A**

2. Refer to the pattern to mark with a pencil or air-soluble marker the spots where the petals attach to the center of the flower. Attach the petals to the flower by guiding the wire through the holes. Adjust the petals to your preferred position, equally spaced and sticking out of the fluffy center. Couching stitch the base of each petal in place. **B**

Finishing

See Displaying Embroidery (page 22) for instructions on how to secure your columbine in a hoop or in a frame. I transferred mine to a 5.7˝ × 7.5˝ (14.5 × 19cm) Nurge oval flexi hoop.

A

B

Emperor Dragonfly

FINISHED PROJECT SIZE: 2˝ × 3½˝ (5.1 × 8.9cm)

The bright and colorful dragonflies that visit our backyard are always a welcome sight. They dazzle with their aerial stunts and iridescent wings, and, importantly, they keep pesky mosquitos at bay! This Emperor Dragonfly explores how nontraditional materials can be used in an embroidery project to create unusual stumpwork elements. Heat-fusible angelina film is combined with wire slips to create wings that catch the light and reflect a range of shimmery colors, just like a real dragonfly.

Materials

Size 10 embroidery needle

1 embroidery hoop, size 4˝ (10.2cm)

Tapestry or other large needle

Graphite paper

Jewelry wire, gauge 24

Wire cutters

Sakura 3D Crystal Lacquer

Craft-quality detail paintbrush

Small, pointed scissors

Electric clothing iron

Towel or parchment paper

Candle

Matches or lighter to light candle

Emperor Dragonfly Pattern (page 159)

Frame for display, optional

Thread and Fabric

1 spool of Kreinik Blending Filament 094—Star Blue

2 squares 7˝ × 7˝ (17.8 × 17.8cm) of Kona cotton in Aqua

2 rectangles 4˝ × 6˝ (10.2 × 15.2cm) of angelina film in Opal

DMC six-stranded cotton embroidery floss (1 skein of each):

STITCHES USED IN THIS PROJECT

Satin Stitch, page 31

Long-and-Short Stitch, page 35

Backstitch, page 29

Seed Stitch, page 29

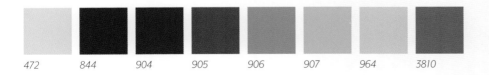

| 472 | 844 | 904 | 905 | 906 | 907 | 964 | 3810 |

Transfer the Pattern

See Transferring Patterns (page 27) for more information.

1. Transfer the body pattern to Kona Aqua fabric, using your preferred method. Layer a second piece of Kona Aqua fabric underneath and secure both layers together in the 4˝ (10.2cm) hoop. **A**

Embroider the Body

The body is stitched with one strand of embroidery floss and a size 10 needle.

1. Fill in the eye with horizontal long-and-short stitches of DMC 904 that curve around the contour of the eye. Add two rows of straight stitches of DMC 964 and 3810 below the eye. Separate the eyes with a straight stitch of DMC 844. Fill in the top of the head with vertical long-and-short stitches of DMC 472. **B**

2. Embroider the legs with straight stitches of DMC 844. **C**

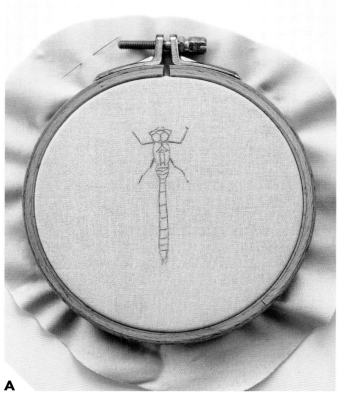

A

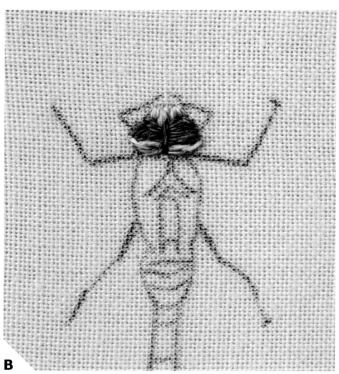

B

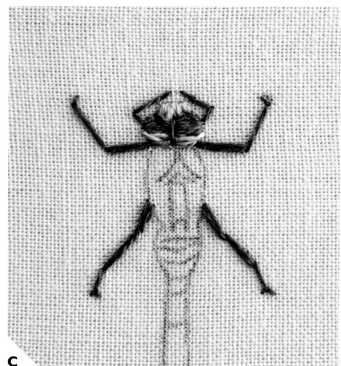

C

3. Embroider the middle of the thorax with long-and-short stitches of DMC 964. Blend DMC 905, 906, and 907 in long-and-short stitches on the sides of the thorax, as shown. **D**

4. Fill in the abdomen with vertical long-and-short stitches of DMC 3810. Add horizontal stripes across the abdomen with straight stitches of DMC 844 to create segments. Stitch the end of the abdomen with four straight stitches of DMC 844. **E**

5. Add iridescent highlights to the right side of the abdomen and the sides of the thorax with straight stitches of Kreinik Blending Filament 094. **F**

D

E

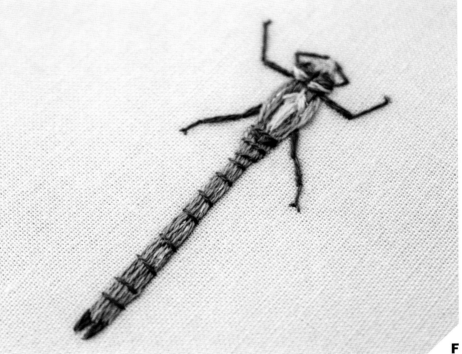

F

Make the Wings

1. Cut four pieces of wire long enough to outline each wing, plus 2˝ (5.1cm) extra each. Refer to the pattern and shape each piece of wire to look like the two hindwings and two forewings. **A**

2. Twist the two ends of each wing. **B**

3. Preheat your iron to the hottest setting. Tape a piece of angelina film to a flat, iron-safe surface. Place all the wire slips on the piece of angelina film. Position the twisted ends outward and securely tape them in place. **C**

4. Place a second layer of film over the first piece of angelina film. Cover the entire wing portion of the wire slips. **D**

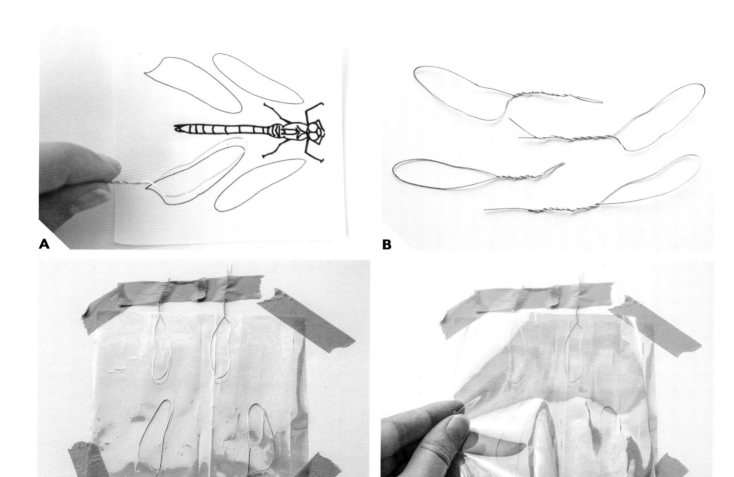

A

B

C

D

5. Cover the layers of angelina film with a towel or piece of parchment paper. Iron the layers of film on high heat for approximately 3–5 minutes, or until they are bonded together. The layers should adhere to the wire slips and not pull apart easily. **E**

6. Cut out each wing and trim up to the edges of the wire. **F**

7. Light a candle. Carefully and slowly move the wing toward the candle flame until the excess film around the wired frame begins to melt away. Do not hold the wing above the flame or get too close, as the film will burn or melt away completely. **G**

8. Repeat Step 7 with the remaining wings. **H**

· FLAMELESS OPTION ·

The candle heat smooths and seals the wings' edges and slightly modifies the colors of the film. If you are uncomfortable working with an open flame in this step, you can opt to carefully trim away the excess film with sharp, pointed scissors and move on to Step 9.

9. Paint each wing with a smooth layer of the Sakura 3D Crystal Lacquer or other clear lacquer. The lacquer adds a clear protective layer to the delicate wings so they do not tear or come apart from their wire frame. Thoroughly wash the paintbrush immediately after, or the bristles will harden as they dry. Allow the wings to dry completely. **I**

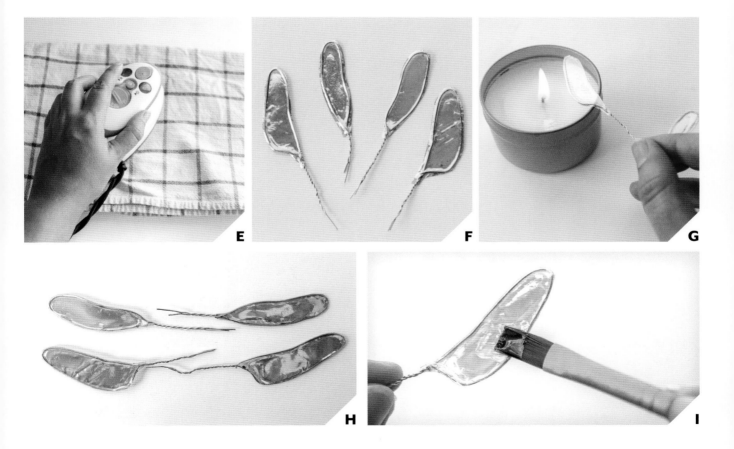

Assembly

See Stumpwork Embroidery (page 46) for more information about attaching the wings to the body with a tapestry needle.

1. Refer to the pattern to mark with a pencil or air-soluble marker the four spots where the wings attach to the body. Use the tapestry needle to make a hole in each spot. Attach the wings to the body by guiding the wire through the holes. Adjust the wings to your preferred position.

Finishing

See Displaying Embroidery (page 22) for instructions on how to secure your dragonfly in a hoop or in a frame. I transferred mine to a vintage mosaic frame.

Broad-Billed Hummingbird

FINISHED PROJECT SIZE: 3¾˝ × 5˝ (9.5 × 12.7cm)

Spotting a hummingbird often feels a bit magical to me. There is something special about these small, brightly colored pollinators. They are the most elusive birds that visit my backyard, and they never seem to dwell very long in one spot. Because they are such a rare sight, I wanted to honor these beautiful little birds by re-creating one to live forever in our home. This project combines thread painting, padded stumpwork, and wire-slip stumpwork to create a Broad-Billed Hummingbird that appears to hover above the frame, ready to flit away to the nearest flower.

Materials

2 embroidery hoops, sizes 7˝ (17.8cm) and 4˝ (10.2cm)

Size 10 embroidery needle

Tapestry or other large needle

Sulky Stick 'n Stitch paper

Graphite transfer paper

Jewelry wire, gauge 24

Wire cutters

Fabric glue

Craft-quality detail paintbrush

Small, pointed scissors

Beeswax thread conditioner

Broad-Billed Hummingbird Pattern (page 158)

Frame for display, optional

Thread and Fabric

2 squares 10˝ × 10˝ (25.4 × 25.4cm) of Kona cotton in Orchid

7˝ × 7˝ (17.8 × 17.8cm) square of Kona cotton in Silver

12˝ × 18˝ (30.5 × 45.7cm) sheet of Benzie wool-blend felt in Ecru

DMC six-stranded cotton embroidery floss (1 skein of each):

STITCHES USED IN THIS PROJECT

Couching Stitch, page 34

Satin Stitch, page 31

Long-and-Short Stitch, page 35

Seed Stitch, page 29

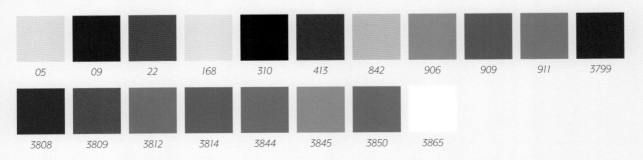

05	09	22	168	310	413	842	906	909	911	3799

3808	3809	3812	3814	3844	3845	3850	3865

Transfer the Pattern

See Transferring Patterns (page 27) for more information.

1. Transfer the wing pattern shape to the Kona Silver fabric, using your preferred method. Secure the fabric in the 4˝ (10.2cm) hoop. **A**

2. Print or draw the body and attached wing pattern onto Sulky Stick 'n Stitch paper. Follow the instructions on the package for your printer type.

3. Cut out the body outline pieces from the Benzie wool felt.

Prepare the Padded Base

1. Secure two layers of Kona Orchid in the 7˝ (17.8cm) embroidery hoop.

2. Couching stitch the felt body outlines #1, #2, and #3 on top of one another, one at a time, to the Kona Orchid base fabric. **B**

3. Peel and stick the pattern on top of the padded base. Align the sticker so the padded base is completely within the lines of the body pattern. **C**

Prepare the Wire Slip

See Stumpwork Embroidery (page 46) for more information.

1. Shape the wire slip around the individual wing. Couching stitch the inner corner of the wire slip with DMC 909. Couching stitch DMC 906 along the top of the wing. Couching stitch the rest of the wire slip with DMC 3865 until the wire is covered completely. **D**

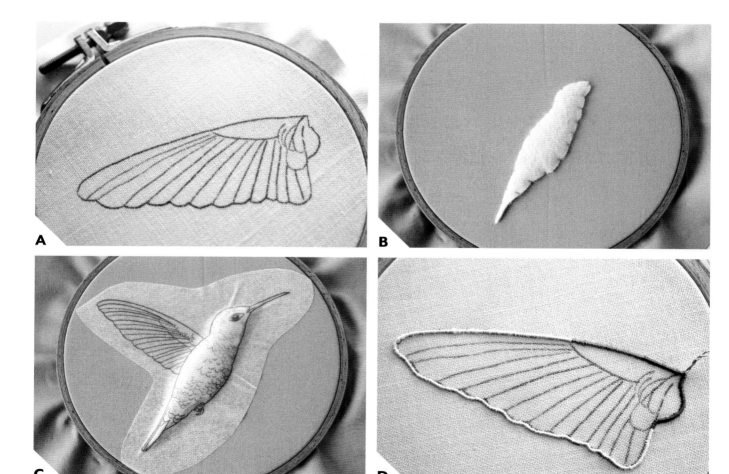

A

B

C

D

Embroider the Wing

This pattern is stitched with one strand of embroidery floss and a size 10 needle unless otherwise specified in the directions.

1. Blend DMC 906 with 3808, 909, and 911 in long-and-short stitches to fill in the corner feathers of the wing. **A**

2. Backstitch the lines between each feather with DMC 168. **B**

3. Fill in each feather of the wing with DMC 168 and 3865 blended in long-and-short stitches. Slightly curve the stitches to show the natural curve of the wing. **C**

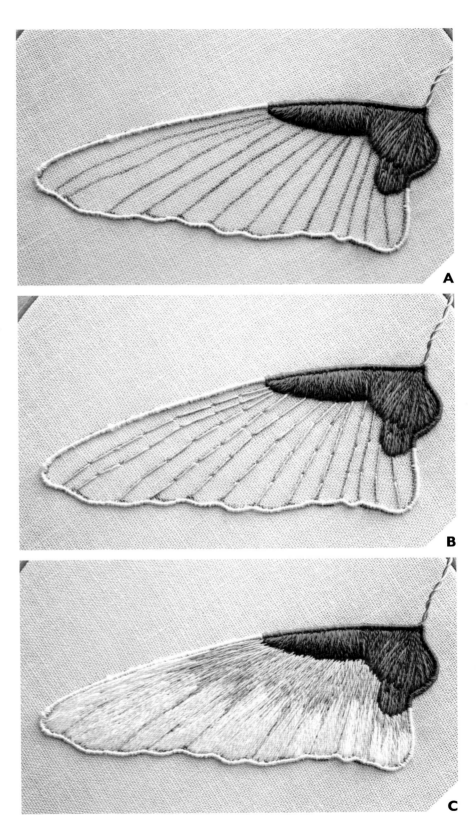

A

B

C

Embroider the Body

Eye

1. Fill in the center of the eye with long-and-short stitches of DMC 310. Add a reflection to the top of the eye with two seed stitches in DMC 3865 and two seed stitches in DMC 168. **A**

> **· EYE REFLECTIONS ·**
>
> *Look closely at your eye in a mirror. You will see elements of the room around you reflected back in your eye's lens. Now, imagine that this hummingbird is real. Its eyes would reflect more than just light. They would reflect a tiny glimpse of their surroundings, like perhaps the colors of a garden. Use more than one color for the eye's reflection to create a more realistic animal eye. Pale purples, blues, grays, and whites are ideal choices to reflect the light and color of an animal's surroundings.*

2. Backstitch around the eye with DMC 05. Keep the stitches as small as possible. **B**

3. Long-and-short stitch the area around the eye with DMC 09 and 842. **C**

Head

1. Embroider long-and-short stitches of DMC 909 from the edge of the beak to above the eye. Fill in the remaining area above the eye with small rows of satin stitches blending DMC 909, 911, and 3850. **D**

2. Fill in the chin with three rows of satin stitches of DMC 3808. Blend straight stitches of DMC 909 throughout the last two rows. **E**

> **· IRIDESCENT FEATHERS ·**
>
> *Hummingbirds' feathers are iridescent due to their unique shape and structure. They reflect light and appear to be multicolored, depending on the angle they are viewed from. Blend the straight stitches of highlight colors freely and at random when embroidering the feathers to re-create the iridescent effect.*

3. Satin stitch a row of feathers in the middle of the head, behind the eye, with DMC 3844. Add a row of satin stitches of DMC 3845 below it. **F**

4. Continue to fill in the neck with rows of satin stitches of DMC 3808. Blend straight stitches of DMC 3812 and 3845 throughout the rows. **G**

5. Fill in the remaining area of the head with satin-stitched rows of DMC 3812 and straight stitches of DMC 909 blended throughout. **H**

Midsection

1. Fill in the underside of the hummingbird with long-and-short stitches blending DMC 3808, 3812, and 3850. Angle some stitches slightly to create a ruffled look. **I**

2. Blend DMC 909, 911, and 906 in long-and-short stitches to fill in the back of the hummingbird. **J**

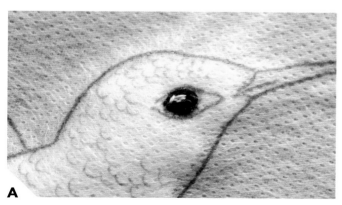

A

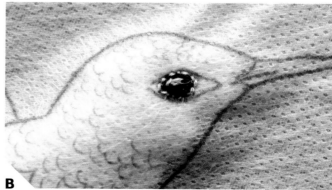

B

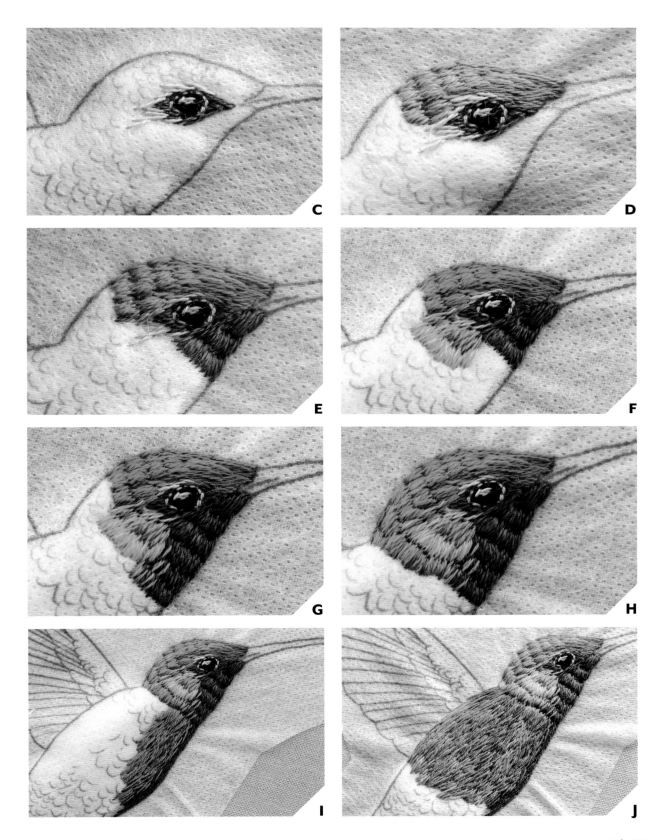

C
D
E
F
G
H
I
J

Bill

1. Blend DMC 22 and 3799 in long-and-short stitches to fill in the bill, as shown.

2. Backstitch a line of DMC 413, bisecting the bill. **A**

Tail

1. Satin stitch rows of DMC 911 along the back and DMC 3814 along the underside of the hummingbird. Vary the sizes of the rows slightly. Angle and lengthen some stitches to give a ruffled look. **B**

2. Blend straight stitches of DMC 906, 909, and 3850 at random throughout the rows of feathers. **C**

3. Blend DMC 842 and 05 in long-and-short stitches to fill in the area around the feet. Overlap and vary the angle of the stitches to create a ruffled look. **D**

4. Fill in the tail feathers with long-and-short stitches of DMC 3808. Blend long-and-short stitches of DMC 3809 to create subtle lines between the three feathers of the tail. **E**

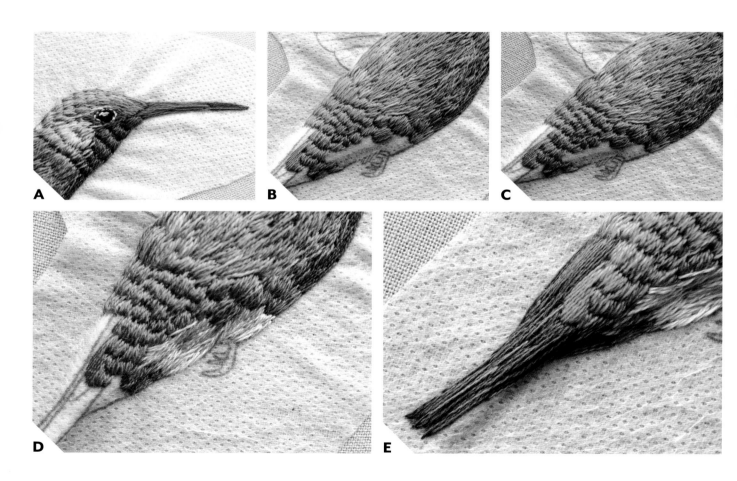

Feet

1. Fill in the feet with straight stitches of DMC 413. Shorten and angle the stitches slightly to accommodate the curve of each toe. **A**

Wing

1. Satin stitch the three upper sections of the wing with DMC 909, 906, and 3809. **B**

2. Backstitch the lines between the feathers with DMC 168. **C**

3. Blend DMC 168 and 3865 in long-and-short stitches to fill in the feathers. **D**

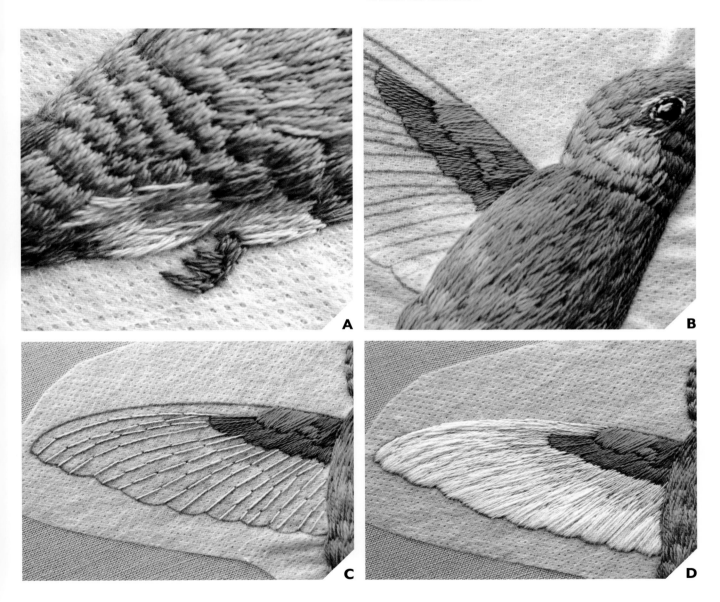

A

B

C

D

Remove the Sulky Stick 'n Stitch Paper

1. Wash away the Sulky Stick 'n Stitch paper completely in warm, soapy water. Rinse thoroughly. Allow the piece to dry completely.

Assembly

See Stumpwork Embroidery (page 46) for more information about cutting out, gluing, and attaching the wing to the hummingbird.

1. Cut away all excess fabric from the wire slip wing. Paint glue onto the backs and edges of the wing. Let the wing dry completely.

2. Refer to the pattern and mark with a pencil or air-soluble marker the spot where the wing attaches to the body. The wing sits slightly below the background wing. Use the tapestry needle to make a hole. Attach the wing to the body by guiding the wire through the hole. Adjust the wing to your preferred position.

3. Couching stitch the wing in place with DMC 909.

Finishing

See Displaying Embroidery (page 22) for instructions on how to secure your broad-billed hummingbird in a hoop or in a frame. I transferred mine to a vintage frame.

ACCESSORY PROJECTS

Dandelion Tote Bag

FINISHED PROJECT SIZE: 5½˝ × 6˝ (14 × 15.2cm)

The common dandelion is such a fun, whimsical flower. My children love making bouquets with the fluffy seed heads and bright, sunny flowers, so these flowers are a sweet reminder to me of summers spent outdoors together. This pattern pairs padded stumpwork with tapestry yarn to give the leaves and flowers subtle dimension and turkey stitches to create the wooly seeds. Stitching with this fluffier yarn makes a bolder statement for an accessory. Embroider this pattern on a linen tote so you can carry some of the magic of these cheerful blooms with you throughout your day.

Materials

2 embroidery hoops, sizes 5˝ (12.7cm) and 9˝ (22.9cm)

Size 18 tapestry needle

Size 10 embroidery needle

White graphite transfer paper

Scissors

Dandelion Pattern (page 159)

Lightweight fusible interfacing, optional

Thread and Fabric

12˝ × 18˝ (30.5 × 45.7cm) sheet of Benzie wool-blend felt in Ecru

Cotton linen tote bag

DMC cotton embroidery floss in any color for attaching felt

DMC tapestry wool yarn (1 skein of each):

STITCHES USED IN THIS PROJECT

Long-and-Short Stitch, page 35

Turkey Stitch, page 32

Backstitch, page 29

Couching Stitch, page 34

Straight Stitch, page 29

| Ecru | 7043 | 7342 | 7344 | 7348 | 7433 | 7435 | 7510 | 7538 |

Transfer the Pattern

See Transferring Patterns (page 27) for more information.

1. Transfer the pattern onto the tote with white graphite transfer paper.

2. Center the flower in the 9˝ (22.9cm) hoop. The dandelion seed part of the pattern does not need to be within the hoop. This part will be embroidered later. **A**

Embroider the Leaves

This pattern is stitched with tapestry yarn and a size 18 tapestry needle.

1. Backstitch the center veins with DMC 7043 for the two bottom leaves and DMC 7348 for the upper four leaves. **B**

2. Embroider the 2 bottom leaves with long-and-short stitches of DMC 7344 and 7342. Begin at the base of the leaf with DMC 7344 and gently angle the stitches outward. Blend long-and-short stitches of DMC 7342 to fill in the rest of the leaf. **C**

> **· UNEVEN EDGES ·**
>
> *Create character and texture through uneven stitches when working with tapestry wool. Change the stitches' direction and size to mimic the rough, uneven edges of the dandelion's leaves.*

3. Embroider the upper four leaves with long-and-short stitches of DMC 7043 and 7344. Blend straight stitches of DMC 7342 in the tips and edges of the leaf. **D**

Embroider the Stem

1. Backstitch the three main stems with DMC 7344 and 7043. Add small straight stitches of DMC 7344 at the top of the stems to form calyxes. **E**

2. Backstitch the stem for the bud with DMC 7342. Add straight stitches to the top of the stem to form the calyx. **F**

A

B

C

D

E

F

Embroider the Flowers

1. Cut the four circles from the pattern in Benzie wool felt in Ecru. Stack circles #1 and #2 on the smallest flower and stack circles #3 and #4 on the largest flower.

2. Thread the size 10 needle with two strands of cotton embroidery floss in any color. Couching stitch the felt padding to the flower heads. **A**

3. Thread the tapestry needle with DMC 7435. Embroider long-and-short stitches that meet in the center of the flower. Blend long-and-short stitches of DMC 7433 around the outside. **B**

4. Embroider the bud with straight stitches of DMC 7435. **C**

5. Turkey stitch the center of the seed head with DMC 7510. Trim and fluff the yarn. **D**

6. Turkey stitch around the center of the seed head with DMC Ecru. Trim and fluff the yarn. **E**

Embroider the Seeds

1. Secure the loose seed shapes in the 5″ (12.7cm) embroidery hoop. **F**

2. Backstitch the bottom of each seed with DMC 7538. Turkey stitch the top of each seed with DMC Ecru. Trim and fluff the yarn. **G**

Finish the Tote

1. Turn the tote inside out. Trim any thread ends to ⅜″ (1cm) inside the tote.

2. Optional: Iron a lightweight fusible interfacing on the backside of the embroidery inside the bag to protect the stitches from being pulled or stretched while the tote is in use.

A

B

C

D

E

F

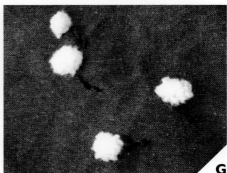

G

Frog and Asters Shirt

FINISHED PROJECT SIZE: 2½˝ × 4½˝ (6.4 × 11.4cm)

Embroidery is one of my favorite ways to upcycle and personalize clothes. Stitch this fun frog and asters pattern on any shirt, jacket, or other clothing item you want to give more color and character. This pattern explores how different fibers can be used for different subjects within the same embroidery pattern to emphasize their distinct features. Tapestry wool, padded stumpwork, and beading give the frog its full shape and bumpy skin texture. Asters are very small, delicate flowers, and so they are embroidered with regular cotton embroidery floss and small seed beads.

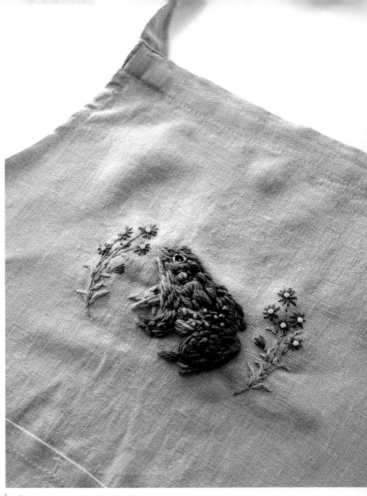

The same pattern embroidered on an apron

Materials

1 embroidery hoop, size 9˝ (22.9cm)

Size 18 tapestry needle

Size 10 embroidery needle

Graphite transfer paper

Scissors

Linen or cotton shirt (avoid stretchy and synthetic materials)

Seed beads in yellow, olive green, and tan brown

Frog and Asters Pattern (page 157)

Lightweight fusible interfacing, such as Sulky Tender Touch (optional)

Thread and Fabric

Cotton or linen shirt or other accessory item

12˝ × 18˝ (30.5 × 45.7cm) sheet of Benzie wool-blend felt in Fern

DMC cotton embroidery floss in shades that match your beads

DMC six-stranded cotton embroidery floss (1 skein of each):

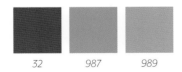

| 32 | 987 | 989 |

STITCHES USED IN THIS PROJECT

Long-and-Short Stitch, page 35

Satin Stitch, page 31

Couching Stitch, page 34

Seed Stitch, page 29

Backstitch, page 29

Straight Stitch, page 29

DMC tapestry wool (1 skein of each):

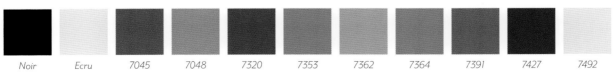

| Noir | Ecru | 7045 | 7048 | 7320 | 7353 | 7362 | 7364 | 7391 | 7427 | 7492 |

| 7622 | 7624 |

Transfer the Pattern

See Transferring Patterns (page 27) for more information.

1. Print or draw the pattern on Sulky Stick 'n Stitch paper. Follow the printing instructions on the package.

2. Cut out the numbered body pieces from the Benzie wool felt.

Prepare the Padded Base

1. Secure the shirt or accessory in the 9˝ embroidery hoop.

2. Thread a size 10 needle with one strand of DMC cotton embroidery thread in any color.

3. Couching stitch the felt body outline #1 to the base fabric. Layer the felt body outline #2 over the first. Couching stitch the piece in place. Couching stitch the felt piece #3 over the back leg area of the body outline. **A**

4. Peel away the back of the Stick 'n Stitch paper. Align over the padded felt outline and adhere to the fabric. **B**

Embroider the Frog

Head

1. Embroider the center of the eye with straight stitches of DMC Noir. Outline the center with straight stitches of DMC 7492. Add 2 seed-stitch highlights to the corner of the eye with DMC Ecru. **C**

2. Embroider long-and-short stitches of DMC 7045 to fill in the bottom half of the head and DMC 7427 to fill in the top half of the head. **D**

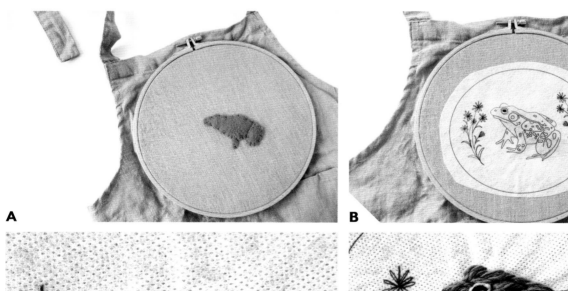

A

B

C

D

3. Seed stitch the nostril with DMC 7624. Backstitch the ridge along the frog's side with DMC 7624. **E**

4. Fill in the frog's ear, the round disk on the side of the head, with straight stitches of DMC 7353 and 7391, as shown. **F**

Midsection

1. Satin stitch the spots on the body with DMC 7624 and 7622. **G**

2. Fill in the midsection below the ridgeline with long-and-short stitches of DMC 7320. Fill in the back above the ridgeline with long-and-short stitches of DMC 7427. **H**

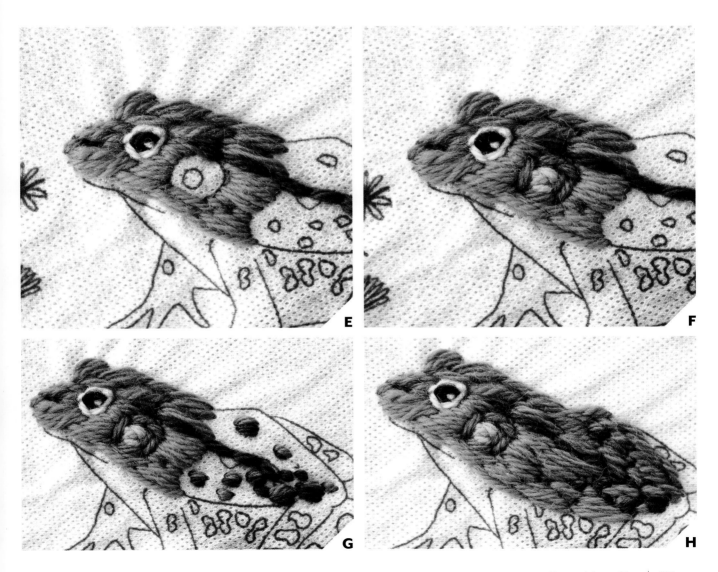

Underside and Legs

1. Fill in the throat with long-and-short stitches of DMC 7362 and 7364, blended. **A**

2. Satin stitch the spots on the legs and underside with DMC 7391. **B**

3. Fill in the front right leg with vertical long-and-short stitches of DMC 7048. **C**

4. Fill in the area between the front and back legs with long-and-short stitches of DMC 7362 and 7364. **D**

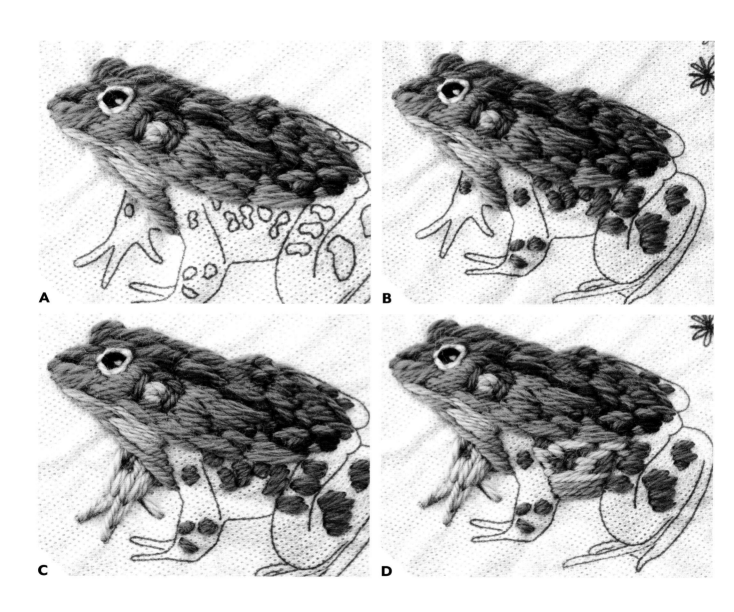

A

B

C

D

5. Fill in the left front leg with long-and-short stitches of DMC 7320. The stitch direction should flow vertically from the top of the leg to the tips of the toes. **E**

6. Embroider the back two legs with long-and-short stitches of DMC 7427. Gradually alter the stitch direction to follow the curves of the limbs. **F**

7. Embroider the web between the back toes with a couple of straight stitches of DMC 7353. **G**

E

F

G

Embroider the Asters

Use a size 10 needle and two strands of cotton embroidery floss for Steps 1–3.

1. Backstitch the stems with DMC 987. **A**

2. Fill in the leaves with straight stitches of DMC 989. **B**

3. Embroider the petals with straight stitches of DMC 32. **C**

4. Gently hand wash the paper away in warm, soapy water. Rinse well and air-dry.

Add Beads

Flowers

1. Thread a size 10 needle with two strands of DMC 973 or a shade of yellow that matches your beads.

2. Bring the needle up next to the center of the flower. Thread the bead onto the needle and pull it down until it rests on the fabric. **D**

3. Bring the needle back down through the center of the flower to secure the bead in place.

4. Repeat Steps 2 and 3 until all open flowers have a beaded center. **E**

> **· FRENCH KNOT ALTERNATIVE ·**
> *Embroider double-stranded French knots at the center of each flower in place of seed beads.*

A

B

C

D

E

Frog

1. Thread a size 10 needle with two strands of DMC 3363 or a shade of green that matches your beads. Add 3–4 olive green beads to the side of the frog.

2. Thread a size 10 needle with two strands of DMC 3860 or a shade of light brown that matches your beads. Add 5–6 light brown beads to the side of the frog.

Finish the Project

1. Trim any thread ends to ⅜" (1cm) on the backside of the shirt or accessory.

2. **Optional:** Iron a lightweight fusible interfacing on the backside of the embroidery to protect the stitches from being stretched or pulled loose while the shirt or accessory is worn.

Buttercup Pendant

FINISHED PROJECT SIZE: 1¾˝ × 1¾˝ (4.4 × 4.4cm)

Buttercups are known for their distinct shining and iridescent petals, a trait designed to attract pollinators. Because they appear to radiate light, these sunny yellow flowers symbolize joy, happiness, and friendship. This pendant would make a great gift for a friend or loved one, or keep it for yourself to wear on days when you want to radiate a bit of sunshine.

Materials

2 embroidery hoops, sizes 4˝ (10.2cm) and 5˝ (12.7cm)

Sizes 8 and 10 embroidery needles

Tapestry or other large needle

Graphite paper

Air- or water-soluble fabric pen

Jewelry wire, gauge 24

Wire cutters

Fabric glue

Craft-quality detail paintbrush

Small, pointed scissors

Beeswax thread conditioner

Buttercup Pattern (page 157)

Superglue

Pendant setting, 4cm

Necklace chain

Thread and Fabric

1 spool of Kreinik Metallic Very Fine #4 Braid 091—Star Yellow

2 squares 9˝ × 9˝ (22.9 × 22.9cm) of Kona cotton in Violet

7˝ × 7˝ (17.8 × 17.8cm) square of Kona cotton in Canary

12˝ × 18˝ (30.5 × 45.7cm) sheet of Benzie wool-blend felt in Fern

DMC six-stranded cotton embroidery floss (1 skein of each):

| 17 | 165 | 726 | 727 |

STITCHES USED IN THIS PROJECT

Couching Stitch, page 34

Long-and-Short Stitch, page 35

Turkey Stitch, page 32

Transfer the Pattern

See Transferring Patterns (page 27) for more information.

1. Transfer the petals to Kona Canary fabric, using your preferred method. Secure the fabric in the 5˝ (12.7cm) hoop. **A**

2. Secure the two squares of Kona Violet fabric in a 4˝ (10.2cm) hoop and trace the outline of the pendant insert on the middle of the fabric with a water- or air-soluble pen. **B**

3. Transfer the flower center pattern to the Benzie wool felt and cut out. Couching stitch it to the center of the pendant outline. **C**

Prepare the Wire Slip

See Stumpwork Embroidery (page 46) for more information.

1. Shape the wire slips to the petal shapes. Couching stitch them with DMC 727 until wrapped completely. Twist the wire ends. **D**

Embroider the Petals

Each petal is stitched with one strand of DMC embroidery floss and a size 10 embroidery needle. The stitch direction starts at the inner corner and follows the curve of the petal.

1. Fill in each petal with a gradient of long-and-short stitches of DMC 727, 17, and 726. **E–F**

2. Use a size 8 needle and Kreinik Metallic Very Fine #4 Braid 091 to blend 8–9 straight stitches of varying length to each petal. **G**

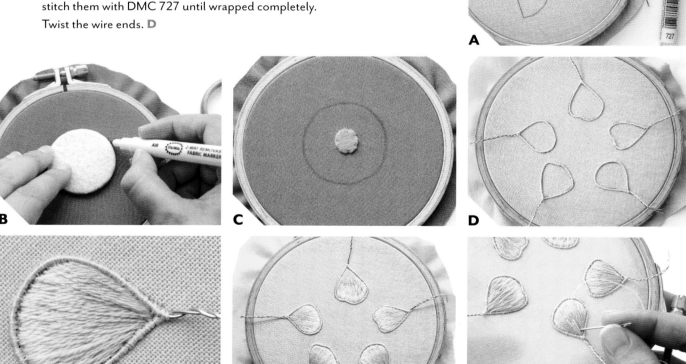

The gradient begins with the darkest color, DMC 726, at the narrowest part of the petal and grows lighter toward the edge of the petal.

Begin each stitch at the narrowest part of the petal and radiate out toward the edge.

Embroider the Flower Center

1. Thread a size 8 needle with 3 strands of DMC 165. Cover the padded felt center with turkey stitches. Trim to create a rounded fluffy flower center. **A**

2. Surround the center with a new row of turkey stitches made with two strands of DMC 17. **B**

3. Trim the outer turkey stitches to about 5mm above the level of the center turkey fluff. **C**

Assembly

See Stumpwork Embroidery (page 46) for more information about cutting out, gluing, and attaching the petals to the center of the flower.

1. Cut away all excess fabric from the stumpwork petals. Paint glue onto the backs and edges of the petals. Let them dry completely. **D**

2. Refer to the pattern to mark with a pencil or air-soluble marker the spots where the petals attach to the flower center. Use the tapestry needle to make a hole in each spot. Attach the petals to the center by guiding the wire through the holes. Adjust the petals to your preferred position, equally spaced and sticking out of the fluffy center. Couching stitch the base of each petal in place. **E**

Finishing

See Displaying Embroidery (page 22) for instructions on how to secure your buttercup in a pendant setting. I used a 1⅝˝ (4cm) hardwood setting from artbase on Etsy for mine.

Cottontail Rabbit Brooch

FINISHED PROJECT SIZE: 1½˝ × 1½˝ (3.8 × 3.8cm)

A sweet cottontail rabbit sits contentedly among summer florals in this miniature thread-painting project. Learn how to add a rich variety of texture and dimension to even the smallest embroideries by combining such techniques as padded stumpwork, thread painting, turkey stitches, and embroidery with specialty fibers, such as variegated threads and silk ribbons.

Materials

1 embroidery hoop, size 4˝ (10.2cm)

Size 10 embroidery needle

Size 18 chenille needle

Sulky Stick 'n Stitch paper

Scissors

Cottontail Rabbit Pattern (page 158)

Miniature hoop setting, such as the 2˝ (5.1cm) acrylic miniature embroidery hoop by Dandelyne

Superglue

1.5˝ (3.8cm) bar pin

Thread and Fabric

DMC Color Variations (1 skein) of 4215

The Thread Gatherer 4mm Silken Ribbons (1 of each) of Desert Moss and Straw into Gold

7˝ × 7˝ (17.8 × 17.8cm) square of Kona cotton in Grasshopper

12˝ × 18˝ (30.5 × 45.7cm) sheet of Benzie wool-blend felt in Ecru

DMC six-stranded cotton embroidery floss (1 skein of each):

STITCHES USED IN THIS PROJECT

Couching Stitch, page 34

Satin Stitch, page 31

Seed stitch, page 29

Long-and-Short Stitch, page 35

Turkey Stitch, page 32

Straight Stitch, page 29

Threading Silk Ribbon, page 28

| 310 | 422 | 433 | 838 | 869 | 948 | 3771 | 3781 | 3790 | 3865 | 3866 |

Transfer the Pattern

See Transferring Patterns (page 27) for more information.

1. Print or draw the body pattern onto Sulky Stick 'n Stitch paper. Follow the instructions on the package for your printer type.

2. Cut out the body outline pieces from the Benzie wool felt.

Prepare the Padded Base

1. Secure a layer of the Kona Grasshopper in the 4˝ (10.2cm) embroidery hoop.

2. Couching stitch the felt body outline to the Kona Grasshopper base fabric. Then, align and couching stitch the felt head and leg pieces to the body outline. **A**

3. Peel and stick the pattern on top of the padded base. Align the sticker so the padded base is completely within the lines of the pattern. **B**

Embroider the Head

This pattern is stitched with one strand of embroidery floss and a size 10 needle unless otherwise specified in the directions. See Miniature Thread Painting (page 56) for more information.

1. Fill in the eye with small straight stitches of DMC 310. Begin at the corner of the eye and angle the stitches to form the curve of the eye. Add two seed stitches of DMC 3865 as a highlight. **C**

2. Fill in the nose area with vertical satin stitches of DMC 3781 and horizontal satin stitches of DMC 3790. **D**

3. Embroider long-and-short stitches of DMC 422 and 3790 around the eye. **E**

4. Blend long-and-short stitches of DMC 869 and 3781 to fill in the rest of the head. **F**

Ears

1. Embroider the inner ear with long-and-short stitches of DMC 3771 and 948, blended. Outline the ear with small, straight stitches of DMC 3790. **G**

2. Embroider the back ear with straight stitches of DMC 3781. **H**

A

B

Embroider the Body

1. Create the shadowed contours of the legs with long-and-short stitches of DMC 838. Add a shadow to the underside of the head as well, along the curve of the neck. **A**

2. Blend long-and-short stitches of DMC 869 and 3781 to fill in the forelegs. Gently curve the stitches downward to create the fullness of the legs. Embroider the front feet with vertical satin stitches of DMC 3790. **B**

3. Blend DMC 869 and 3781 in long-and-short stitches to fill in the side of the rabbit between the forelegs and hindleg. **C**

4. Fill in the hindleg with long-and-short stitches of DMC 869. Blend long-and-short stitches of DMC 422 around the curve of the leg to create a ruffled look. Embroider the back foot with horizontal satin stitches of DMC 3790. **D**

5. Fill in the underbelly with long-and-short stitches of DMC 3781. **E**

6. Turkey stitch the tail with DMC 3866. Trim and fluff the threads. **F**

Hydrangea

1. Thread a size 10 needle with two strands of DMC Color Variations 4215. Fill in the 3 circles of the hydrangea pattern with French knots. **G**

> **· FRENCH KNOT SIZES ·**
>
> *Vary the number of times the thread is wrapped around the needle, between one and three times, to create knots of different sizes. A combination of larger and smaller knots creates depth in the hydrangeas.*

A

B

C

D

E

F

G

Sunflower

1. Satin stitch the inner circle of the sunflower pattern with DMC 433. Turkey stitch around the inner circle with DMC 838. Trim into a fluffy ring. **A**

2. Hand wash away the Sulky Stick 'n Stitch paper with warm water. Air-dry the project completely. The silk ribbons used in the final steps are delicate and should not be washed.

3. Thread a chenille needle with 4mm yellow silk ribbon, such as The Thread Gatherer Silken Ribbon in the shade Straw into Gold.

4. Embroider straight stitches around the center of the flower to create the petals. **B**

Leaves

1. Thread a chenille needle with 4mm green silk ribbon, such as The Thread Gatherer Silken Ribbon in Desert Moss.

2. Embroider straight stitches on either side of the hydrangeas and sunflower to create leaves. Vary the angle and length of the stitches to create different size leaves. **C**

Setting the Finished Embroidery

See Displaying Embroidery (page 22) for instructions on how to secure your cottontail rabbit embroidery in a setting. I secured mine in a 2˝ (5.1cm) clear acrylic miniature embroidery hoop by Dandelyne. I attached a 1.5˝ (3.8cm) bar pin with superglue to the back of the hoop so I could wear it as a brooch. **D**

A

B

C

D

Robin's Nest Ring

FINISHED PROJECT SIZE: 1″ × 1″ (2.5 × 2.5cm)

Birds are nature's fiber artists, weaving intricate and beautiful nests from a variety of carefully curated materials. I have long been inspired by these utilitarian yet artistic nests, which led me to explore different threads and fibers in my own work. Like a real robin's nest, this tiny embroidered nest is created with natural fibers, slowly assembled layer by layer. This project shows you how to work with a variety of textures to create dramatic depth and visual interest on an embroidery with even the simplest stitches.

Materials

1 embroidery hoop, size 4˝ (10.2cm)

Size 18 chenille needle

Mat board or cardboard

Scissors

Ring setting

Superglue

Thread and Fabric

Wiltex Threads Vineyard Silk in C129 Smokey Taupe

The Thread Gatherer Sea Grass (cotton) in Tudor Brown

The Thread Gatherer Sea Grass (cotton) in Prairie Grass

The Thread Gatherer Oriental Linen (linen) in Aged Barnwood

The Thread Gatherer Shepherd's Silk (wool/silk blend) in Dark Moss

The Thread Gatherer 4mm Silken Ribbons (silk) in Aqua Clouds

The Thread Gatherer Sanibel (kid mohair) in Cape Chestnut

Rainbow Gallery Wisper (kid mohair) in W89—Ecru

7˝ × 7˝ (17.8 × 17.8cm) square of Kona cotton in Silver

12˝ × 18˝ (30.5 × 45.7cm) sheet of Benzie wool-blend felt in Ecru

STITCHES USED IN THIS PROJECT

Straight Stitch, page 29

Turkey Stitch, page 32

Couching Stitch, page 34

Threading Silk Ribbon, page 28

Prepare the Padded Base

1. Cut a piece of cardboard or mat board to fit the inside diameter of the ring setting. This piece of board will be used later to mount the finished embroidery in the setting. **A**

2. Secure a layer of Kona cotton in Silver in the 4˝ (10.2cm) embroidery hoop.

3. Measure and cut two felt circles the same size as the cardboard piece. Cut out the center of each circle to create an O-shape. **B**

Embroider the Nest

There is an element of untidiness to even the most carefully crafted robin's nest, as bits of grass, twigs, and other materials poke out in different directions. Vary the length and direction of your straight stitches to create a more realistic and natural-looking nest.

1. Align the two pieces of felt on top of each other and the base fabric.

2. Thread the chenille needle with one strand of the Vineyard Silk Smokey Taupe thread, or similar dark brown silk thread. Embroider straight stitches around the two layers of felt to anchor them to the fabric base. **C**

> **· FINISHING OFF ENDS ·**
> *Rather than tie off the end of your thread on the backside when you are done with a color, pull the remaining thread back up through the nest and trim it to about 5mm in length. The loose thread end mimics the look of a loosened twig, poking out from the nest.*

3. Thread the chenille needle with a strand of The Thread Gatherer Sea Grass in Tudor Brown. Straight stitch around the perimeter of the nest. Repeat with The Thread Gatherer Sea Grass in Prairie Grass. Leave gaps between stitches to accommodate other fibers. **D**

4. Thread the chenille needle with a strand of The Thread Gatherer Oriental Linen in Aged Barnwood. Fill in the remaining gaps with straight stitches around the perimeter of the nest. **E**

5. Thread the chenille needle with a strand of The Thread Gatherer Sanibel in Cape Chestnut. Fill in the inner cup of the nest with short stitches. Begin at the outer perimeter of the nest's cup and make short stitches around the interior until reaching the center. **F**

6. Thread the chenille needle with a strand of Rainbow Gallery Wisper in W89 and add 5–6 straight stitches to the inside of the cup at random. This mohair is very wispy and, in this piece, mimics feathers. **G**

Embroider the Eggs

Straight stitches with ribbon are executed the same as with regular cotton embroidery thread. The effect is a full, smooth stitch with pointed ends—perfect for a small robin's egg.

1. Thread a chenille needle with the 4mm silk ribbon in Aqua Clouds.

> **· RIBBON LENGTH ·**
> *Keep your working ribbon length 8˝ (20.3cm) or shorter. Silk ribbons are also prone to fraying when pulled through fabric repeatedly, and a shorter length reduces repeated friction on the ribbon and potential waste.*

2. Within the cup of the nest, bring the ribbon up to the front of the embroidery where you want to start the egg.

3. Pierce the needle back down through the fabric where you want the egg to end. **H**

4. Place your finger between the fabric and ribbon to keep the ribbon smooth and untwisted as you pull it through the fabric. **I**

5. Leave some lift to the ribbon rather than pull it taut. Gently lift, adjust, and smooth the ribbon with the blunt end of the needle, as needed.

6. Repeat Steps 2–5 to create additional eggs in the nest. A 25mm nest can accommodate up to 4 or 5 embroidered eggs. I embroidered three silken eggs in my nest, as a reminder of my own three children. **J**

· VARIATIONS ON NESTS ·
I have embroidered this pattern several times, making small adjustments each time to create a wholly unique nest. For a magpie's nest, I add straight stitches of shiny metallic threads and golden seed beads to the nest's exterior. I also change the color of the eggs and the amount or color of fluff lining the nest's cup to mimic other bird species' nests. This pattern is very versatile and leans heavily on your creativity, so I hope you have fun exploring different ways to alter it.

Embroider the Moss

1. Thread the chenille needle with The Thread Gatherer Shepherd's Silk in Dark Moss.

2. Turkey stitch patches of moss around the perimeter of the nest at random. Trim and fluff to create a mossy texture. **K**

Setting the Finished Embroidery

See Displaying Embroidery (page 22) for instructions on how to secure your nest in a jewelry setting. **L**

The finished nest is laced to the cardboard insert before it is glued in its final woodland-inspired 25mm ring setting.

TEMPLATES

BEARDED IRIS

MONARCH BUTTERFLY

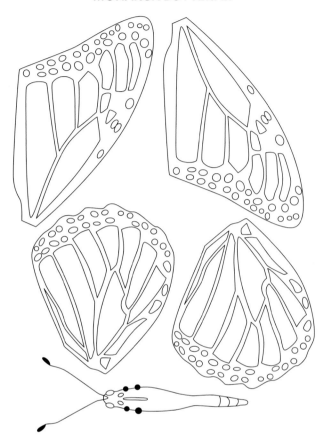

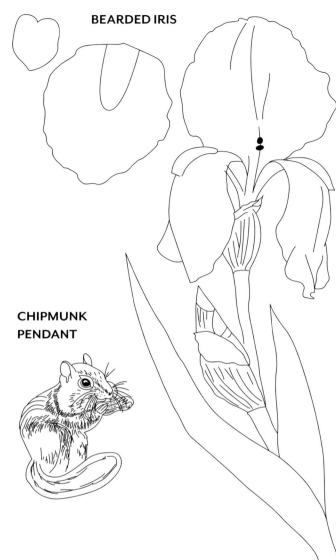

CHIPMUNK PENDANT

WHITE-TAILED BUMBLEBEE

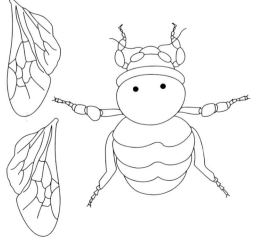

COLUMBINE FLOWER

BUTTERCUP
PENDANT

MALLARD
DUCKLING

FROG AND ASTERS SHIRT

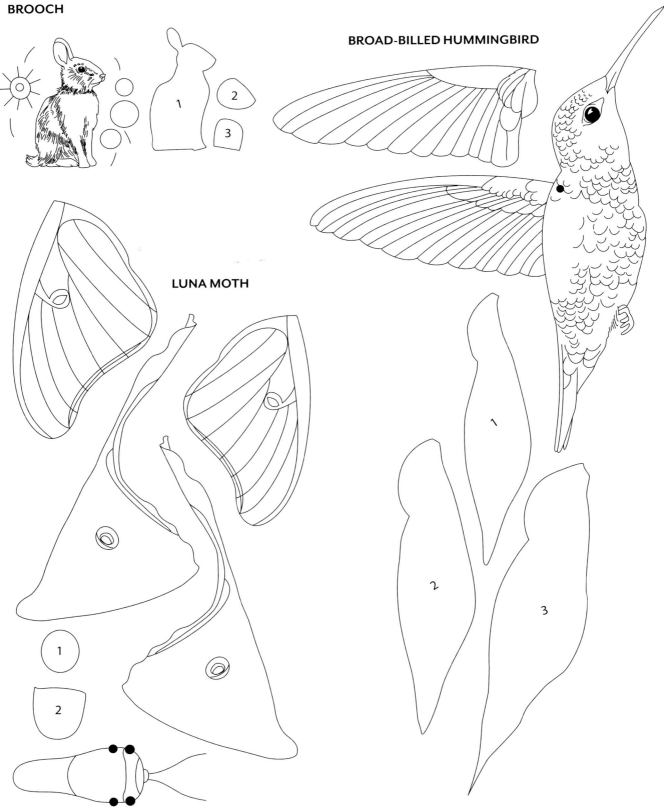

COTTONTAIL RABBIT
BROOCH

BROAD-BILLED HUMMINGBIRD

LUNA MOTH